The Solar Eclipse of October 2014

Its Impact on the Markets

Tim Bost & Jim Cummins

FinancialCyclesWeekly.com

Harmonic Research Associates

The Solar Eclipse of October 2014: Its Impact on the Markets

Submit all requests for reprinting to:
Harmonic Research Associates
611 Riviera Dunes Way, Unit 702
Palmetto, FL 34221 USA

The astrological and market charts in this publication were prepared with the Fibonacci/Galactic Trader software from PAS Inc. (www.galacticinvestor.com) and the Solar Fire, Solar Maps, and Nova Chartwheel programs available from Astrolabe (www.alabe.com).

Published in the United States of America by Harmonic Research Associates.

www.HarmonicResearchAssociates.com

Paperbound Edition

ISBN-10: 1-933198-50-8
ISBN-13: 978-1-933198-50-7

EAN: 9781933198507

Solar Eclipses and Market Activity

As we consider the final solar eclipse of 2014, we are clearly in the midst of a time of massive global transformation. The polarization between political, religious, and cultural factions has reached new heights of acrimony, bitterness, and self-serving hypocrisy. The gap between the haves and have-nots at opposite ends of the economic spectrum has been expanded to an unprecedented degree, with understandable amplifications of anger, resentment, and disillusionment taking deep roots in the public consciousness.

That economic polarization has also been increasingly expressed on a global scale as well, with the BRICS nations openly defying Western power blocs and creating the rudiments of their own economic infrastructure, with Balkan factions shedding blood as they try to define and defend geopolitical boundaries that determine access to and control over key energy resources, and with a Chinese holding company overpowering Wall Street with the brute force of a wildly popular Initial Public Offering capitalized at a quarter of a trillion dollars.

While all of these developments were clearly foreshadowed by the solar eclipse in April, 2014, their pervasiveness and power on the world stage was certainly unanticipated and unprecedented. When we look at solar eclipses we are definitely dealing with matter of global consequence, and international events like the ones that have taken place in the past six or seven months can serve as as a salutary reminder of just how powerful eclipses really are. At the same time, as we look to the markets as bellwethers of emerging trends in the broader social and geopolitical arena, we have an additional opportunity to enrich our understanding of the real power of eclipses and of the huge potential that lies ahead.

As is so often the case, as we anticipate the coming of the next solar eclipse, already experiencing the kind of tension, stress, and turmoil that can so often be triggered by high-impact astrological events. In our personal and we are all grappling with personal professional relationships, in our financial traumas and unfulfilled priorities, with fantasies and hopes about our prospects for the future, and with massive uncertainty provoked by global tensions, social unrest, and the hysterical sensationalism of the mass media, which simultaneously manages to trivialize the true significance of cooperative initiatives and technological advances while fanning the flames of myopic xenophobia in a maelstrom of preoccupation with personalities and petty scandals.

It's undoubtedly a dangerous and disturbing situation, and since solar eclipses act as intense focal points for the full range of our experience, we can inevitably expect many of our world's major dissonances, injustices, and other problematical circumstances to get increasing emphasis during the coming months.

In spite of that distressing context, however, the solar eclipse on October 23 offers us a rare ray of optimism, should we be willing to look past stereotypes and allow some serendipitous grace into our perception of the world around us. The solar eclipse of October 23 is likely to mark a time of important endings as well as new beginnings, giving us a genuine opportunity to welcome new paradigms into our consciousness. If we're willing to take that risk in the face of oppositional thinking, artificial limitations, and outright hostility, we're likely to be quite surprised at the outcome in our personal and social lives, in our financial and economic well-being, and in our individual spiritual and intellectual development.

While the solar eclipse in October 2014 provides us with an excellent opportunity for embracing a new perspective in our lives and with afocal point for comprehending the current turmoil in our neighborhoods and around the global, and while that eclipse is the primarily subject of this monograph, it's important to remember some of the specific planetary dynamics that have set the stage for the current circumstances that we are confronting in the markets, in the economy, and in the broader contexts of our lives.

One of the biggest and most important factors underlying the current intensity of planetary alignments is the Cardinal Climax, which began in 2008 and will continue to make its influence felt at least through 2015. This historic emphasis on transformation and new beginnings is the result of outer planets moving into the early degrees of the cardinal signs of the zodiac-- Aries, Cancer, Libra, and Capricorn.

These planetary ingresses have not only been activating these degree areas for an extra emphasis on the initiation of new ideas, new types of activity, and entirely new social paradigms; they have also formed fourth-harmonic connections with what is known as the "World Point" in the Hamburg School Uranian system of symmetrical astrology-- the specific zodiacal zones that create global importance for mundane events.

The net implication of the Cardinal Climax is that we are truly at the birth of a new era in human experience and a new level of consciousness for the planet as a whole. The solar eclipse of October 2014, like each solar eclipse during the 2008-2015 time frame, gives an opportunity to crystallize that consciousness in a material form, anchoring our intuitive and spiritual insights in pragmatic, down-to-earth affairs.

While that opportunity to redefine our paradigms for personal and social experience can be invigorating, it also has a potentially challenging side if we are involved in the markets. After all, one of the biggest mistakes we can make in the markets is to convince ourselves that "this time it's different" when we look at market trends and cycles. Although astrological phenomena and their corresponding dynamics in the markets do in fact come to us in a never-ending stream of unique combinations, the behavior of the markets is far more likely to follow precedents and to behave in predictable ways than it is to create circumstances that have never been seen before.

As we look at the solar eclipse in October 2014 against the backdrop of the Cardinal Climax, then, our task is to balance our awareness of innovation and the potential for far-reaching shifts in societal, governmental, and commercial structures with methodical attention to the patterns, rhythms, and divergences that create exceptional opportunities in the markets, especially in the context of the conflicts and confrontations that can strain the social and geopolitical fabric.

Conflicts and confrontations are an especially important part of the mix of opportunities and challenges facing all of us right now, primarily because of the continuing role of the series of waxing Uranus/Pluto squares which began in 2012 and which will continue into mid-2015. This extraordinarily powerful planetary alignment has already had a massive impact on geopolitical structures around the globe, and the underlying attitude of intense opposition and brinkmanship that it fosters in nations, political parties, religious groups, and individuals with a strong commitment to a particular ideology or to a sense of personal mission is something that we can expect to intensify for the next couple of years.

In the case of the solar eclipse of October 2014, however, it's especially important for us to take the Uranus/Pluto square series into account. The last Uranus/Pluto square occurred on April 21, and the next square in the series will arrive on December 15. The October 23 solar eclipse is thus exactly 77.7% of the distance between the two Uranus/Pluto events, immediately bringing to mind the strange significance of the 37th harmonic and its degree equivalents in zodiacal calculations. The position of the October eclipse also resonates quite strongly with the horoscope for the first Uranus/Pluto waxing square in the current series, which took place on June 24, 2012 – it activates the midponts of the Sun and Admetos (ultraconservative energies) and of the Moon and Hades (hours of suffering, worry, and anguish) in the chart for that Uranus/Pluto event.

While much of the significance of these astrological connections is likely to remain veiled to the uninitiated observer, it's nevertheless sufficient for us to note that the solar eclipse in October has a powerful connection with the entire cycle of Uranus/Pluto waxing squares, adding enormously to the high-stress potential for the months and years immediately ahead of us.

But like any time of severe stress, the things that create big conflicts can also create big chances for advantageous activities. With an atmosphere of extreme tension and potentially dangerous confrontation continuing to be a dominant theme in social and political interactions, and with the October 2014 solar eclipse acting as an intensifying focal point, we have a volatile combination that can produce big swings in the movements of the markets, surprising opportunities for traders and speculators, and the potential for developing astro-trading strategies that can be extraordinarily profitable. And as we shall see as we look at the October solar eclipse in greater detail, there are unusual dynamics occurring at the time of the eclipse that promise remarkably beneficial outcomes if we are willing to launch new initiatives in our personal lives, in our commercial endeavors, and in our global relationships. In fact, this solar eclipse has the potential to usher in a new era of prosperity, harmony, and progress, especially for the United States of America.

In short, then, this eclipse is clearly a major astrological phenomenon that deserves some highly-focused consideration, and that's the purpose of this monograph—to provide useful perspectives that we can put to work in our planning, not only at the time of the eclipse itself, but for the months ahead as well, especially when it comes to our involvement in the markets.

The fact of the matter is, we can't escape eclipses and their potent impact on our lives. Throughout human history, these cosmic events have been surrounded with a unique mystique that has inspired superstitions, given birth to myths and legends, and energized folklore, popular culture, and spiritual traditions around the world.

Among the various celestial phenomena which are observable from earth, eclipses are perhaps the most commonly recognized by the general public. They are certainly easy enough to observe with the naked eye, as long as you're in the right place at the right time and you aren't dealing with cloudy or overcast skies.

But the widespread awareness of eclipses is also at least partly due to the fact that when eclipses are visible in a particular locality they typically receive a considerable amount of special attention in local newspapers and on the television news. Usually the news stories and commentaries about eclipses play them up as extraordinarily rare events, sometimes in ways that generate more misunderstanding than useful information.

And that's not all. In recent years, the popular craze for vampire stories in books, movies, and television has stimulated a desire for "pop occult" subjects in general and has morphed on occasion into a variety of eclipse motifs as well. Yet in spite of this somewhat naïve popular awareness (or perhaps because of its amplifying effect in the public consciousness) eclipses somehow carry a special aura of power and magic that is literally awe-inspiring, regardless of the specific cultural context in which the eclipses are considered.

But eclipses are not only mysterious and fascinating events; when properly understood from an astrological perspective and then skillfully used in an active engagement with the markets, they can be powerful money-making tools, too!

Throughout my many years of working with astrology and the markets, I have repeatedly found that eclipses are the single most significant celestial phenomena that we need to reckon with in financial forecasting and market timing. Even so, using eclipses in forecasting presents a unique set of complexities for astro-traders and for market analysts who want to add astrology to their set of tools for prognostication.

About 20 years ago, when I began a systematic study of solar eclipses as key factors in stock market forecasting, I naïvely thought that a simple list of procedural rules and interpretive guidelines would be sufficient to provide the basis for profitable eclipse trading strategies.

Ultimately, however, that proved to be far from the actual case.

A set of rules and guidelines and a well-orchestrated approach to analysis are certainly useful, but during the years that I've been working with eclipses in the markets those rules have gradually evolved, transforming themselves into something quite different from my original guidelines. As a result I've had to rethink my assumptions about eclipses and their effects repeatedly, which overall has been a good thing.

I've repeatedly had to challenge my own prejudices and have been obliged to reexamine traditional astrological texts in the light of more modern empirical studies. While there have been times when I've been left with more questions than answers, for the most part I've actually found those occasions uniquely satisfying. At least those experiences have helped me stay more conscious of exactly what I'm doing while making my own trading decisions, and along the way my forecasts have become more accurate and my trading has become more profitable.

The real challenge is that the original rules and guidelines, along with the assumptions behind them, were based on a limited range of real-world practice. When I first started out I was new to the markets, and there were many things I didn't understand. But the more I have had to deal with diverse experiences in the markets, and the more those real-world experiences have challenged my preconceptions, the more I have come to understand that while eclipse interpretation rules may be important for evaluating behavior and for clarifying our expectations about the potential outcome of events before and after solar eclipses, those rules are not necessarily universally applicable.

Eclipses occur regularly and with great predictability, but each eclipse has its own unique characteristics, and in spite of the fact that there may some fundamental similarities among them, not all eclipses have the same effects on society and on trading activities in the markets.

While the nuances and variations among eclipses certainly make for interesting study and reflection for scholars intrigued by the subtleties of astrological theory, they also present some very real challenges for market astrologers and astro-traders.

Naturally enough, the impulse of most individuals who start to apply astrological considerations to market analysis is to believe that they should simply look for key astrological signatures that connect with the markets in significant ways—after all, if there is a clear relationship between a particular event in the heavens and a corresponding event in the markets, and if that correlation takes place without exception regardless of the specific market trends and circumstances, we will not only have validated astrology as an essential part of technical analysis; we will have discovered the Holy Grail of market forecasting!

Unfortunately, though, things aren't quite that simple in market astrology. There are many nooks and crannies to be explored and many rabbit trails to follow when we start trying to figure out how planetary alignments relate to market action, with inevitable challenges along the way. And in my experience, nothing reveals the obstacles and inconsistencies more quickly than the study of solar eclipses and their impact on the markets.

While different eclipses do have some factors in common, and while there are also eclipse series that link individual eclipses through extended periods of time, each individual eclipse also has its own distinctive characteristics—its own path of visibility, its own position in the zodiac, and its own particular relationship to previous eclipses and to the pattern of planets in the sky at the time the eclipse takes place.

In my own work I have found that it is through an examination of these unique features, especially from an astrological perspective, that we can gain some of the best insights into the potential effects of a particular eclipse. And it's those insights that can help us position ourselves appropriately as astro-traders for optimum profits from our trading in equities, options, and commodities.

The Track Record

Before specifically examining the October solar eclipse for 2014 in detail, however, I think it's worthwhile to review some of the results of the forecasts based on the previous solar eclipse, on April 29, 2014. While forecasting market action based on eclipses is inevitably more an art than a science, it's nevertheless interesting to use an analytical eye in taking a retrospective look at the accuracy of what those forecasts revealed.

I must confess, though, that sometimes that kind of examination is quite humbling because of the errors and misconceptions it reveals—astrologers are human, too, after all, and I've certainly made my share of mistakes (some of them quite embarrassing!). Those errors have been due in most cases to the limits of my own vision and imagination rather than to any shortcomings of astrology itself.

At other times, of course, reviewing previous forecasts and the track record of events that followed them offers some delightful surprises-- every once in a while, the forecasts are actually right! But regardless of whether the track record itself is positive or negative, reviewing it is always instructive, and the insights gleaned from looking at past forecasts always help the current forecasting process as we move ahead to consider the next eclipses that are coming up.

The primary focus in reviewing the forecasts in the last eclipse report, of course, is its accuracy in describing conditions in the stock market. And, as it turned out, those forecasts were well worth paying attention to. Here are a few examples:

In discussing the implications of the horoscope for the April eclipse in relation to the chart for the New York Stock Exchange, I noted that "The upside for large caps may be surprising" for many traders and investors. For much of the time following the April eclipse, the unstoppable vitality of the bull market has confounded many market pundits, embarrassing a lot of stubborn bears along the way.

Even so, in looking at the September 12, 2014 lunar return to the April solar eclipse, we commented that "The markets are going to have a tough time keeping anything that looks like a rally going in late September and early October." With the markets declining by nearly 4 percent between September 19 and October 1, that certainly proved to be case.

It's worth noting that lunar returns to solar eclipses continue to be a particularly effective tool for market forecasting. For example, in discussing the potential impact of the first lunar return to the April solar eclipse, on May 26, 2014, we observed a high "potential for extreme volatility in the trading environment during the weeks that follow this lunar return," and said that from that date until late June "the surprising twists and turn of the market are likely to produce even more surprising reactions and counter-moves along the way." As it turned out, the S&P 500 gained more than 2.6% in the two weeks immediately following the lunar return, then promptly lost about 0.69% in the next few trading days, only to finish out that lunar return cycle with an additional gain of 1.28%.

Our analysis of the impact of the April solar eclipse on Gold trading suggested that “we may see a dampening of retail interest in the yellow metal, especially since acquiring the physical metal requires a considerable capital outlay, pricing many small-scale investors out of the picture.” We also warned that the months following the April eclipse were likely to bring a “treacherous trading environment” for Gold, indicating that “we can be confident that active behind-the-scenes interventions and manipulations will continue to be major factors in the pricing of this metal in the marketplace.”

As any frustrated Gold Bug knows, the yellow metal has not performed very well during the past six months or so. In fact, the price of Gold has dropped by about 13% since late March, 2014.

In our last eclipse report, we were honored to have included mundane astrological analysis by Jim Cummins, whose insights on Vladimir Putin, the Ukraine, and Syria have proven to be extraordinarily accurate. Jim is a frequent contributor to our website at FinancialCyclesWeekly.com, and we're pleased to include his analysis in this monograph as well.

While there are other examples of accurate forecasting in our last eclipse report, we won't belabor the point here-- our work over many years has repeatedly demonstrated the true value of astrology in helping us understand the likely trend of future events.

Besides, the real reason we publish these special reports just prior to each solar eclipse is to help you devise effective trading and investment strategies for the coming months, so what we are most concerned about is how helpful we have actually been in creating tangible trading results.

The Eclipse Trade Track Record

In addition to the analysis of the solar eclipses and Eclipse Lunar Returns during the April 2014 eclipse cycle, there were also four specific stocks mentioned in connection with that solar eclipse that I thought offered good trading prospects: Autoliv, Inc. (ALV), First Bancorp (FBNC), Royal Caribbean Cruises Ltd. (RCL), and Teleflex Incorporated (TFX).

In each case, the proposed trading strategy was "to put on a long position soon after the eclipse takes place. This is typically within a couple of weeks following the eclipse (in some cases waiting for price pull-backs where appropriate for optimum purchasing opportunities). Our plan is to trail a stop if a trade turns profitable, and then, if we are still in the trade, to reevaluate our positions around July 27, 2014, when we will get the Sun's conjunction with the April/October two-eclipse midpoint."

As is so often the case with our solar eclipse trading strategies, the result was a 100% winning trade percentage. In all four cases, this trading strategy proved to be effective, with the stocks we correctly identified as good trading candidates returning an average of 5.93% profit.

As is typically the case with our eclipse-trading strategies, these turned out to be relatively short-term swing trades rather than long-term market positions. Even so, we held these positions longer than is often the case in our swing trading, with the exposure to the markets averaging 34.5 trading days. Here's a quick review of all four of the trades for these "eclipse picks", detailing the entry and exit points, along with the results for each of the trades.

Autoliv, Inc. (NYSE - ALV)

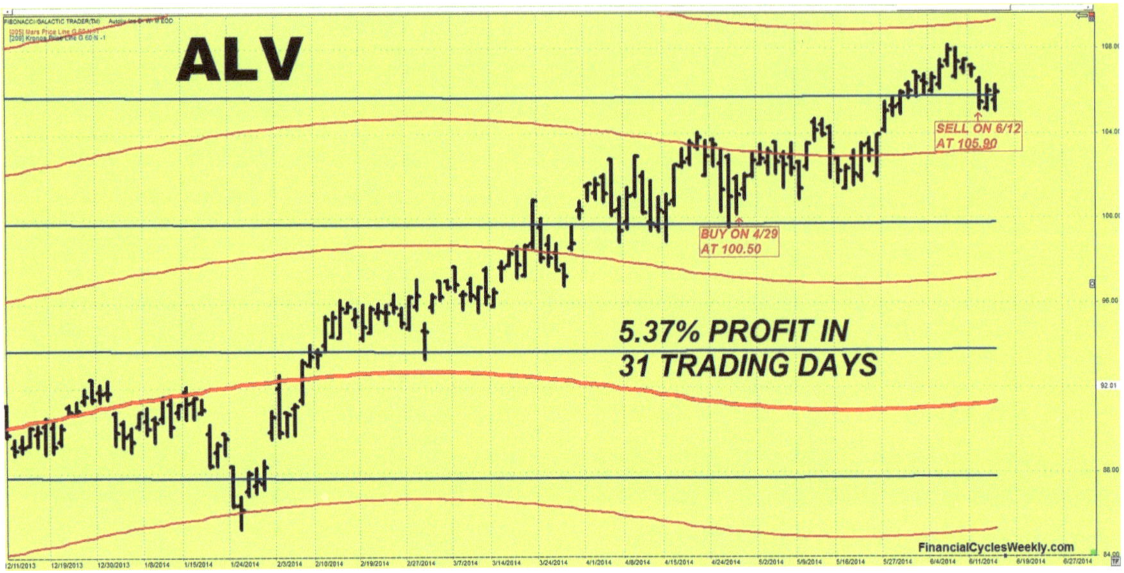

This trade provided a good demonstration of the power of the eclipse trading strategy. We bought ALV on April 29 at 100.50, setting our initial stop at 97.50. On May 2 ALV closed at 102.80, and we raised our stop to 100.75, immediately locking in a profit for the trade. On May 9, with the stock at 101.39, we pushed our stop up to 100.80. By May 16 ALV had started to recover with a close at 102.20, and we raised our stop to 100.85. After the stock had surged up more aggressively to close at 103.93 on May 23, we brought our stop up to 101.25. Another big move took ALV to 106.00 on May 30, and we responded by raising our stop to 104.00. When ALV closed at 107.92 on June 6, we raised our stop to 105.90. That's where we stopped out on June 12, selling ALV at 105.90 for a 5.37% profit I 31 trading days.

First Bancorp (NASDAQ - FBNC)

Bank stocks rarely make dramatic price moves, and this trade was no exception. It was the longest-running of our trades following the April solar eclipse, but it also brought us the lowest return. We bought FBNC on April 29 at 17.25, with an initlal stop set at 16.25. FBNC closed at 17.45 on May 2, and we adjusted our stop to 16.45. With a close on May 9 at 17.76, we raised our stop to 16.60. FBNC dropped back to close at 17.50 on May 16, but we decided to tighten up our stop, raising it to 16.75. We raised that stop to 16.90 after the stock rebounded and closed at 17.87 on May 23. When FBNC closed at 18.08 on May 30, we raised our stop to 17.00. The stock pulled back again at that point, closing at 17.90 on June 6, and we tightened up our stop to 17.10. After a further decline to 17.68 on June 13, we moved our stop to 17.20. We finally locked in a profit for the trade on June 20, when we raised our stop to 17.50 after FBNC had closed at 18.33. The stock dropped back to close at 18.10 o June 27, and we raided our stop to 17.65. The stock's pre-holiday move to a close at 18.53 on July 3 gave us an opportunity to raise our stop to 18.00. That's where we closed the trade, selling FCNC at 18.00 on July 7 for a 4.35% profit in 47 trading days.

Royal Caribbean Cruises Ltd. (NYSE - RCL)

This trade brought our best return from any of our solar eclipse trades. We bought RCL on April 29 at 51.75, with an initial stop set at 49.65. When the stock closed at 53.00 on May 2 we raised our stop to 50.20. RCL then dropped back sharply to close at 51.37 on May 9, and we tweaked our stop to 50.40. The stock closed at 51.90 on May 16, and we brought our stop up to 50.60. A big surge brought RCL up to a close at 54.21 on May 23, and we immediately locked in profits on the trade by moving our stop up to 53.00. When RCL closed at 55.29 on May 30, we raised our stop to 53.50. A further move brought the stock up to a closing price of 56.80 on June 6, and we responded by raising our stop to 55.75. That's where we closed the trade on June 12, selling RCL at 55.75 for a net profit of 7.73% in 31 trading days.

Teleflex Incorported (NYSE - TFX)

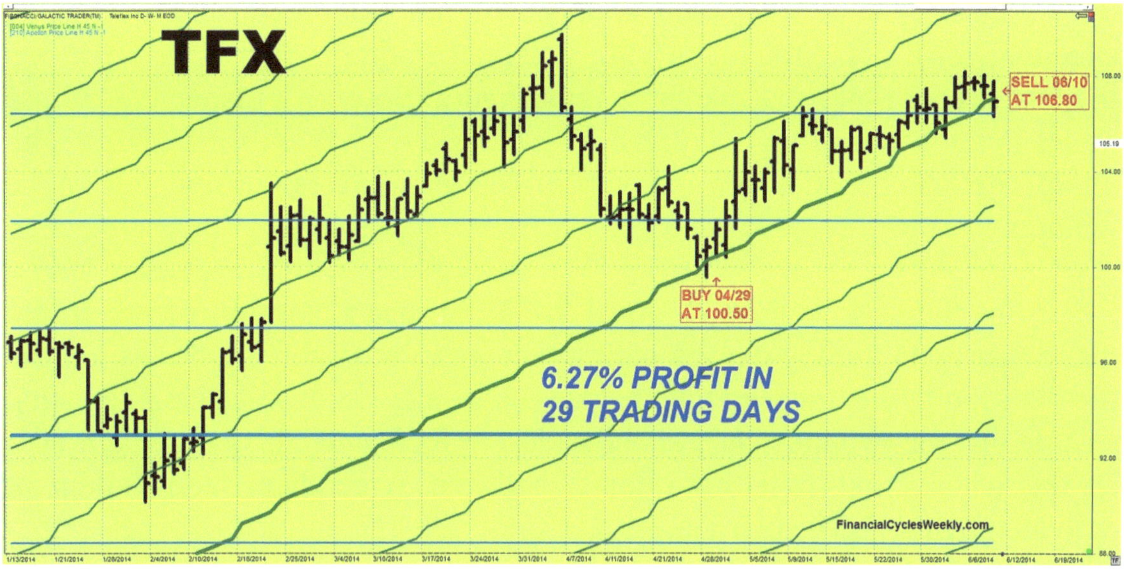

Our eclipse-based trade in TFX began on April 29, when we bought the stock at 100.50. Our initial stop for the trade was set at 99.00. TFX closed at 103.96 on May 2, so we responded by raising our stop to 100.35. When the stock moved up to close at 105.08 on May 9, we were able to lock in profits on the trade by moving our stop up to 102.75. The stock rebounded and moved higher to close at 105.29 on May 23, giving us an opportunity to take our stop to 103.75. We moved that stop up to 105.00 after TFX closed at 106.64 on May 30. The stock gained even more ground to close at 107.75 on June 6, so we raised our stop at that point to 106.80. That stop was hit on June 10, taking us out of the position at 106.80 for a profit of 6.27% in 29 trading days.

Our Overall Trading Results

Once again a study and analysis of the solar eclipse provided an excellent focal point for identifying potential trading opportunities. During the last twelve times that we have published a group of prospective eclipse trades in our series of monographs, we have had only five losing trades, with all of the other trades for the various eclipse cycles turning out to be winners.

For the solar eclipse of April 2014 the mean duration of our trades was a nearly 35 trading days, a period that was almost three times as long as the duration of the trades in the previous eclipse cycle. It was also interesting to note that the two most successful trades, in RCL and TFX, were both with stocks whose first-trade horoscopes had the Ascendant/Hades midpoint activated by the April solar eclipse.

The Final Solar Eclipse of 2014

The second of the two solar eclipses of 2014 comes on October 23, with the Sun and Moon meeting at 0° Scorpio for the event. Because our primary bias in this report is toward the impact the eclipse will have on market activity, especially the activity in the U.S. markets, most of our financial charts in this report are set for New York City, with the eclipse occurring at 17:56:38 p.m. EDT on Thursday, October 23, 2014.

The October eclipse is a partial solar eclipse which will be visible throughout North America except for northeastern Canada, as well as eastern Asia and the northeastern portion of the Pacific Ocean. It comes two weeks after a total lunar eclipse, visible from Antarctica, Australia, Oceania, the Pacific Ocean, Central America, North America, the western part of the Atlantic Ocean, Greenland, and most of Asia and South America.

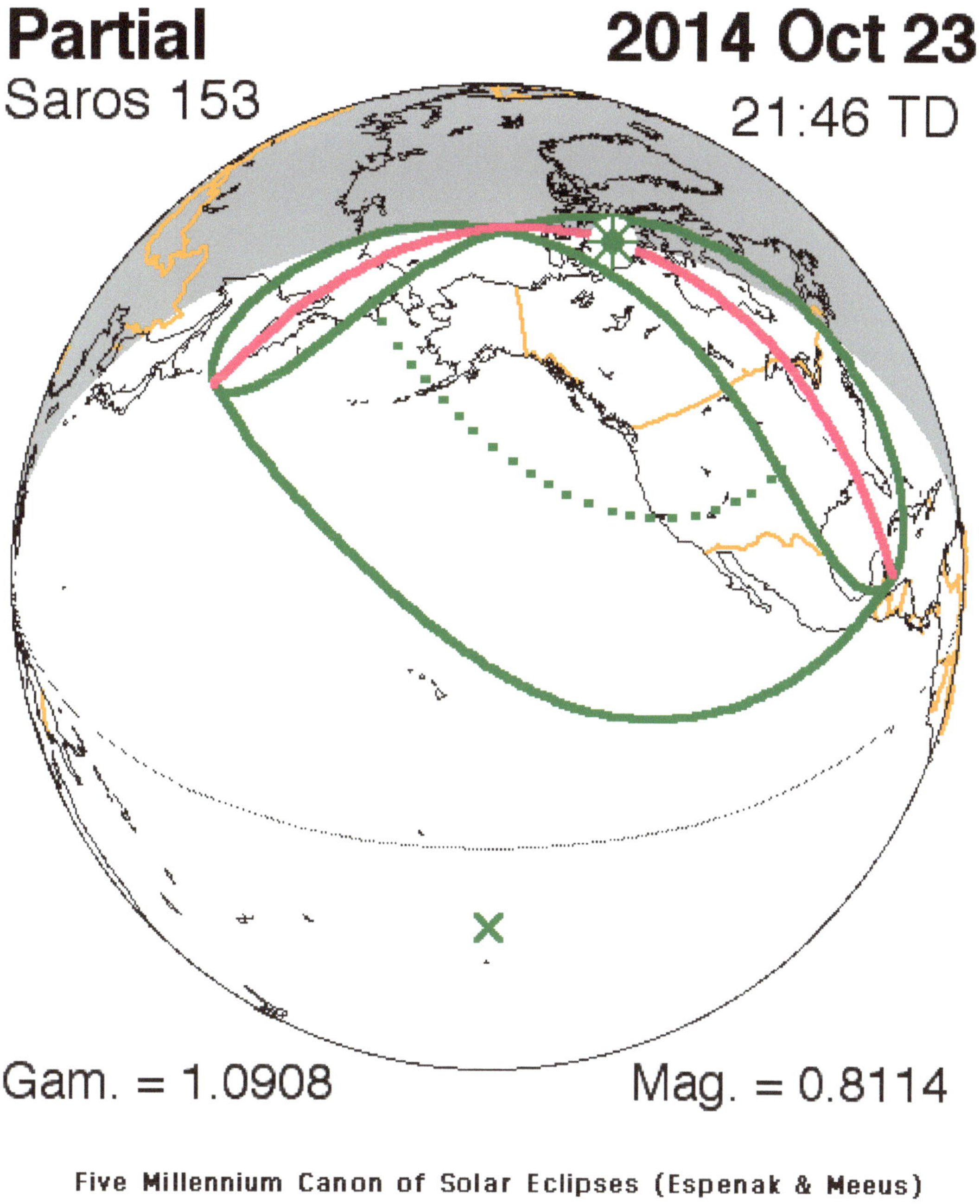

PATH OF PARTIAL SOLAR ECLIPSE – OCTOBER 23, 2014

The October 23 eclipse is a partial eclipse of the Sun located in the zodiac at 00° 25' Scorpio. The eclipse begins as the shadow makes the first contact with Earth at 19:37 GMT, with the event concluding more than four hours later as the shadow leaves the Earth at 23:52 GMT. The time of the greatest eclipse comes at 21:44 GMT, but as astrologers we focus on the New Moon point of Sun/Moon conjunction, at 17:56:38 EDT.

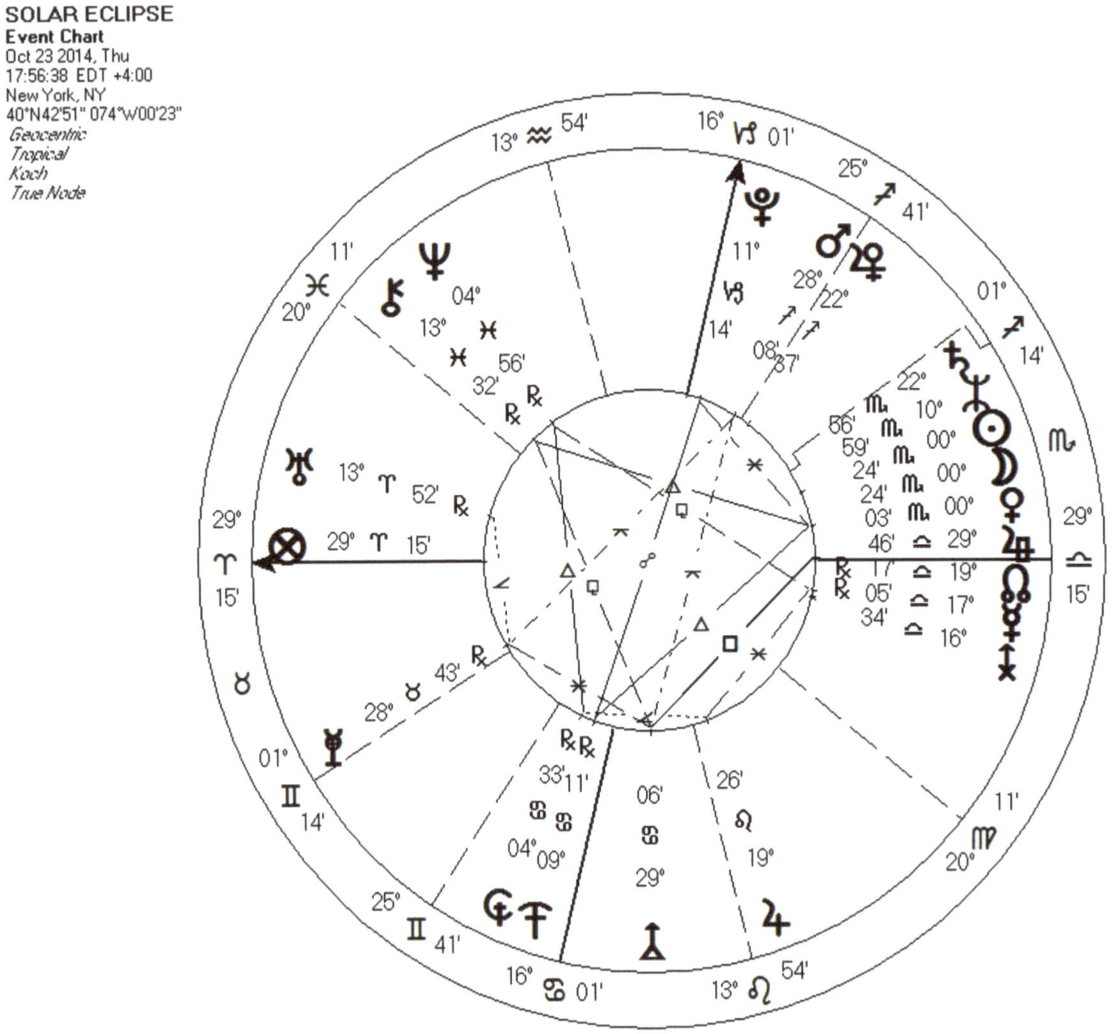

When we look at the October solar eclipse horoscope set for the center of market activity in New York City, we note that the eclipse itself, which takes place near sunset in that location, is posited in the seventh house of the chart. This suggests that above all else, this solar eclipse is about the the importance of partnerships and relationships in general, both personally and globally. With Venus in a precise conjunction with the eclipse, the emphasis is on refinement, love, and artistic expression within the context of relationships, so we can expect to see a push toward greater harmony, cooperation, and respect in the months following the eclipse. It's interesting to note as well that Venus is one of the traditional "money planets" in horoscope configurations, and because the eclipse and Venus also conjoin the transneptunian factor Apollon at 29°46' Libra, there's also a focus here on the expansion of technology and commerce, with an understanding that cooperation and fairness can bring about highly profitable outcomes.

From an astrological perspective, however, there is much more to be considered in chart for this solar eclipse. The transneptunian Vulcanus is square the eclipse point, so even though we can expect a quest for harmony, there are plenty of explosive potentials and latent hostilities lurking in the background. The dominant planetary configuration in the eclipse horoscope is a Yod or "Finger of Fate" pattern formed by Mars in Sagittarius, Vulcanus in Cancer, and Admetos in Taurus. This potent alignment signals an abrupt cessation of efforts, which could manifest as work stoppages, strikes, or the abandonment of major projects. But it can also signify the end of conflicts, an act of surrender, or a permanent cease-fire in a war. Although the potential for events of that sort is revealed here, the eclipse will have a long-lasting effect, and we may not see events associated with this alignment happening immediately after the eclipse itself; they may not be completely evident until the Summer Solstice in 2015. Nevertheless, the seed is being planted now for an ultimate time of cooperation.

Remember, though, that this eclipse is set against the backdrop of a time which is being dominated by massive planetary stress. The waxing Uranus/Pluto square which is at the heart of the configuration is just one of seven such events in a series that began in 2012 and will continue into 2015. Such fourth-harmonic Uranus/Pluto alignments are typically accompanied by times of dramatic belligerence, international conflict, and overt hostilities between individuals, social groups, and political parties. This current 2012-2015 series has been no exception, to say the least.

At the time of the October solar eclipse, the Uranus/Pluto waxing square is not precise, but Uranus is in retrograde motion as Pluto moves forward, bringing the two planets ever closer to their next exact line-up in December. So even though the eclipse encourages reconciliation and harmony, they may be hard to achieve by those set on bitter intransigence.

A potential key to the ultimate outcomes we will see lies in the Mercury/Jupiter sextile in the horoscope for the solar eclipse, with Mercury in the sixth house in Libra and Jupiter in the fifth house in Leo. Although Mercury is in retrograde motion at the time of the eclipse, this alignment is a clear indication of the need for greater communication. Mercury's sixth house position suggests that efforts at forming cooperative connections will need to become persistent and regular operations if they are to meet with success, while Jupiter's fifth house location tells us that greater risks must be accepted if we want to expand our potential for open harmony. Those risks may be the act of communication itself, but in any case the more that parties are willing to take chances at this time in opening up an arena of mutual trust, the more likely they will be to come to agreements which can be mutually profitable, whether the negotiations are taking place on a personal, corporate, or international level. We should note, however, that the energy of the sextile represents opportunities that are entirely optional, so whether or not we actually experience enhanced communications will depend upon the initiative taken by people of good will in the months ahead.

Some of the challenges to bringing about a harmonious situation are revealed by the semi-square that Jupiter forms with Hades at the time of the eclipse. This planetary combination suggests extensive financial losses, but also the potential for successful applications of raw materials. With Hades activating the Cupido/Zeus midpoint, we may find that new enterprises or innovations in mining or in some other development of raw materials may come into sharp focus during the months following the eclipse.

That activation of the Cupido/Zeus midpoint by Hades is also indicative of extremely anti-social behavior, with the potential for extremist groups becoming increasingly belligerent in their efforts to completely annihilate an existing social order. The potential for violent disruption shouldn't be underestimated here, since the additional activation of the Aries/Kronos midpoint by Hades hints of widespread deprivation and severe economic restrictions for large numbers of people in the months following the eclipse.

The role of Mercury in opening up new horizons of cooperation also has a potentially distressing dimension. At the time of the October solar eclipse Mercury activates the Hades/Apollon midpoint, so we can expect widespread discussions about poverty, economic restrictions, and epidemics, as well as public examinations of past policies and historic scientific concepts. There's also a likelihood that important secrets will be revealed during the months after the eclipse, an event which may or may not promote greater levels of trust and understanding.

While there is much in this horoscope to suggest a coming time of enhanced trade and commercial cooperation, the fact that Uranus activates the Mars/Apollon midpoint in the eclipse chart suggests that there will be sudden disruptions in commercial ventures, which could leave the door open for radical new paradigms to find expression in the commercial sphere. Above all, however, this solar eclipse indicates a time of enhanced wealth and prosperity, as is evidenced by the fact that the eclipse itself precisely activates the Jupiter/Pluto midpoint in the eclipse horoscope. This is an indication not only of big money and high finance, but also of the potential for expanding happiness, contentment, and well-being. Let's hope that the current leaders in business and geopolitics respond to this opportunity in creative and pragmatic ways, so that we can all welcome a time of shared abundance.

Although there are many astrological tools for understanding this eclipse, it's perhaps best to set aside obvious and superficial considerations in order to dig beneath the surface of events for maximum material, societal, and spiritual advantage. While love, harmony, and refinement represent core virtues which may seem to be totally foreign to effective and profitable behavior in the markets, nothing could be further from the truth. When we apply astrology to the markets we can simultaneously glimpse the majestic patterns which drive the celestial harmonies behind the movements of the markets, and observe within ourselves the kind of equanimity and intelligence that can help us trade successfully.

The bottom line is this: as astro-traders we will have many potentially profitable opportunities during the months ahead, but taking advantage of those opportunities may not be easy. Effective trading always presents us with major challenges, but as we look at the prospects presented by the partial solar eclipse in October we can surmise that the months ahead require an attitude of consistent caution and persistence as well as an unusually high level of consciousness, emotional balance, and trading discipline if we are to be successful in the markets. Our job is to use advance knowledge of this eclipse to inspire greater dedication, more intense concentration, and a willingness to go the extra mile in serving humanity as we reach new heights in our own personal success.

As always, however, one of our goals with this report is to provide a broader perspective for astro-traders, one that takes into account a more comprehensive range of historical and cultural implications accompanying the current planetary dynamics that are likely to impact the markets. By understanding the astrological mega-trends which operate in the background to shift cultures and consciousness, we can be more finely attuned to the day-to-day opportunities presenting themselves in the markets today.

One of the key factors in understanding the historical perspective of the current eclipse is an awareness on the role in a sequence of eclipses known as a Saros cycle. The solar eclipse on October 23, 2014 is a part of Saros Series 153, a sequence of eclipses that began in the year 1870 with a series of partial solar eclipses that will continue through 2086, followed by annual solar eclipses from 2104 through 2970, and then another series of partial solar eclipses from 2988 through the final eclipse in Saros Series 153, which will be a partial solar eclipse on Augst 22, 3114.

By examining the initial solar eclipse in Saros Series 153, we can begin to get an understanding of the full potential that's provided by the solar eclipse of October 23, 2014 as it impacts world affairs and their relationship to the markets in ways that offer us trading opportunities.

While the events associated with a previous eclipse will not, of course, be exactly duplicated in the months to come, they will at least give us a general idea of what we can expect as we confront the challenges and embrace the opportunities that lie ahead of us. And as we identify specific astrological connections between the horoscope of the solar eclipse that began this Saros Series and the chart of the solar eclipse that lies just ahead of us, we can also refine our expectations and our strategies for dealing with the markets and with the impact of world events.

So let's take a brief look at the solar eclipses that have been a part of Saros Series 153 so far, beginning on July 28, 1870.

PARTIAL SOLAR ECLIPSE – JULY 28, 1870

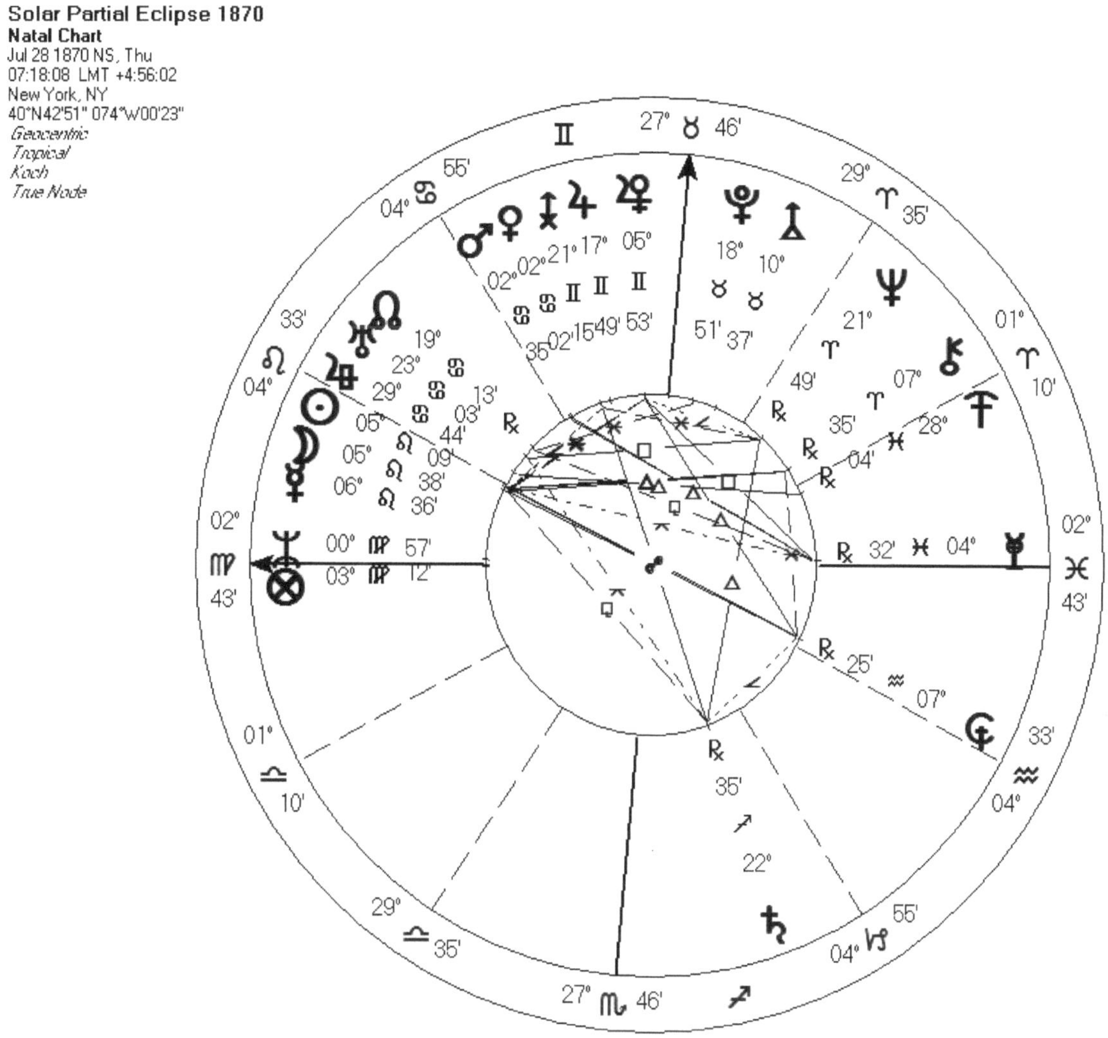

This particular Saros series is especially interesting because it is relatively new, at least in comparison to many of the other sequences of eclipses that we have examined in recent years. The first solar eclipse in the series came on July 28, 1870, just a few days after the Vatican Council voted to accept the Pope as infallible whenever he defines doctrines of morals or faith ex cathedra. This move to consolidate the power of Pius IX and to strengthen the influence of Rome was the result of extraordinarily skillful political moves by the papacy, with papal nuncios strong-arming the Council of Bishops to grant their consent to the doctrine of papal infallibility.

Although 1870 was the year in which the 15th amendment to the U.S. Constitution was ratified, forbidding denial of the right to vote on account of race, color, or previous condition of servitude, this push toward civil liberty was is at best a timid counterpoint to the demands of religious absolutism.

The specific time surrounding this 1870 solar eclipse was noteworthy because of the financial turmoil that accompanied it, with a currency run provoking dramatic central bank action on Thursday, July 28, the precise date of the solar eclipse. On Saturday, July 30, 1870, the ***Investors Chronicle and Money Market Review*** of London reported on this action by the Bank of England by noting that "We have this week to chronicle some important movements in the Money Market, the result of the disturbance occasioned by the War.

"The advance in the Bank rate of discount from 3 to 3 ½ per cent. on Thursday, the 21st inst., having had no influence in checking the outflow of gold, on Saturday, the 23rd, a further movement to 4 per cent. was made. Notwithstanding this step, daily shipments of large amounts of specie to the Continent continued, and there was withdrawn from the Bank, between Saturday and Wednesday last, inclusive, as much as £682,000. At the same time the unsettled state of the Discount Market, where the quotations for good bills were fully ½ and in some cases 1 per cent. above the charge at the Bank, caused a very heavy demand to be threwn upon that establishment. Accordingly, the directors were compelled to adopt further protective measures, and on Thursday last a fresh advance of 1 per cent. in the minimum was announced, thus making the increase in one week from 3 to 5 per cent. This is a sharp movement, but in times such as the present a decided policy is best.

"The Bank action as already had a good effect. A much more settled feeling was apparent in discount circles yesterday, and the quotations no longer exhibited those wide margins which were noticed in the early part of the week. Three months' bills were taken freely yesterday at 5 ½ per cent., with occasional transactions as low as 5, the present Bank minimum, while full six months' bankers paper was negotiated at 5 ½ per cent.

"An earlier tendency will probably soon begin to be manifested. Speculation and new enterprise, if not entirely extinct, will be controlled and kept within a very moderate compass, and the ordinary commercial demand for money, small as it has been for a long time past, will be still further diminished; while, on the other hand, the comparatively high rates now offered for deposits will attract money from the provinces and thus increase the supplies in the discount market. The stock of bullion held by the Bank of England, notwithstanding the recent withdrawals, still amounts to as much as £19,252,490; and it is probable that the further sums required for export will be met to a great extent by the large supplies that are coming forward from America and elsewhere."

With the eclipsed Sun as the final dispositor of this horoscope, and with Venus and Mars in a tight conjunction which is trine restrictive Admetos in the chart, it's little wonder that the start of this Saros series was marked by a time of extreme dogmatism and financial disruptions. Even so, no solar eclipse is entirely negative in its influence and implications, and we can see positive elements in the horoscope for the solar eclipse. For example, Apollon, at 29°44' Cancer in the 1870 eclipse chart, activates the midpoints of Mercury/Uranus (revolutionary thoughts and sudden long-distance communications), Neptune/Hades (unrealized hopes for the future), and Kronos/Poseidon (widespread knowledge and general enlightenment).

While these alignments are significant, they become even more important when we look at the eclipse of July 1870 in the light of the current solar eclipe on October 23, 2014. At the time of the 2014 eclipse, Apollon will be at 29°48' Libra, precisely square the 29°44' Cancer position of Apollon in 1870 at the time of the July solar eclipse. This aspect not only connects the two eclipses; it also opens the door for further positive dynamics because of the mitigating effect that the 2014 eclipse produces in its interaction with the two most negative factors in the 1870 solar eclipse – Cupido conjoins the 1870 Saturn, creating opportunities for creative cultural and social structures which can enhance communication and understanding, while Neptune conjoins the 1870 Admetos, opening up imagination, broader visions, and deeper spirituality in the face of dogmatic expressions and doctrinaire prohibitions. In short, the 2014 eclipse not only maintains the key signature of the original eclipse in this Saros series; it also amplifies that energy in potentially creative and constructive ways.

PARTIAL SOLAR ECLIPSE – AUGUST 7, 1888

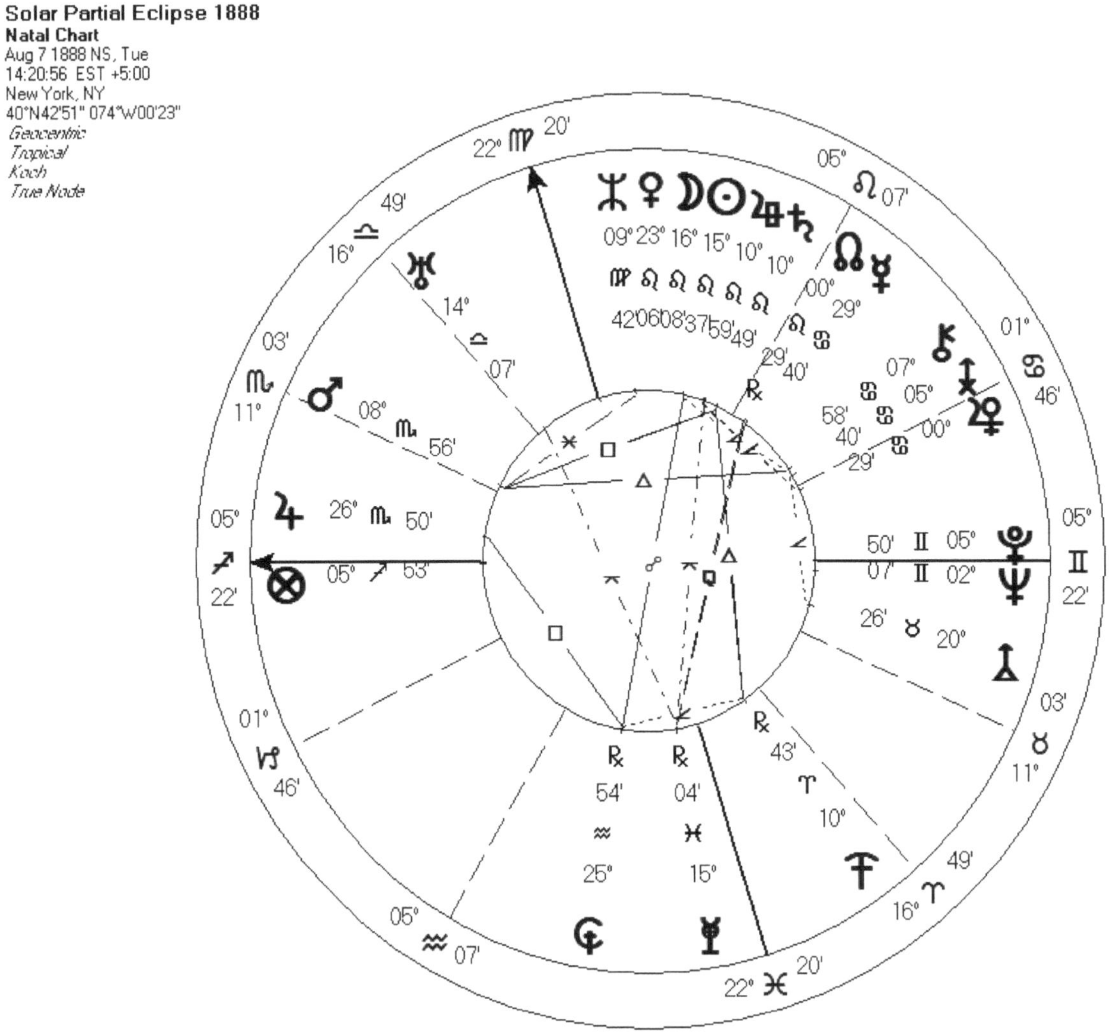

The horoscope for the solar eclipse of August 7, 1888 is remarkable because the conjunction of Saturn and Apollon, suggesting a strong inhibition of expansionary forces, forms a square to Mars, dispositor of Jupiter and a commanding force in the chart.

Three months prior to this eclipse, Brazil completed a set of laws emancipating all the country's slaves, and in the United States the creation of the Department of Labor and the Interstate Commerce Commission helped level the playing field in providing economic opportunities.

1888 was also the year of significant breakthroughs in technology and communications, with Nicola Tesla producing an alternating current electric motor; with William Seward Burroughs of St. Louis acquiring a patent for the world's first successful adding machine; with David Gestetner introducing the first typewriter stencil in London; with the Parker pen company getting started in Janesville, Wisconsin; and with George Eastman introducing the Kodak camera with a promise that “You Push The Button, We Do The Rest”.

Even so, 1888 had its share of xenophobia and social tensions as well, with anti-Chinese riots sweeping Seattle and the U.S. Congress passing a Chinese Exclusion Act less than two months after the solar eclipse.

On the date of the solar eclipse, August 7, 1888, the published average of 12 mixed stocks in the U.S. Closed at 85.67. Six months later, on February 7, 1889, that index closed at 87.71, for a net gain in the interim of 2.38 percent.

PARTAL SOLAR ECLIPSE – AUGUST 19, 1906

The Mercury/Mars conjunction in Leo, in a quincunx to the conjunction of Saturn and Hades in the chart for the solar eclipse of August 19, 1906, provides an important trigger for political and economic dynamics.

It was an extremely eventful time. 1906 was the year that an earthquake left San Francisco influence, providing a massive blow to the American psyche and to the economic push for Western expansion.

It was also the year that a world diplomatic conference revised the Geneva Convention of 1864, and that the All-India Muslim League was founded by the Aga Khan. The U.S. War Department began excavation work on the Panama Canal, and the first Grand Prix motorcar race was organized in France. Just one month after the solar eclipse, a major typhoon hit Hong Kong, killing over 50,000 people.

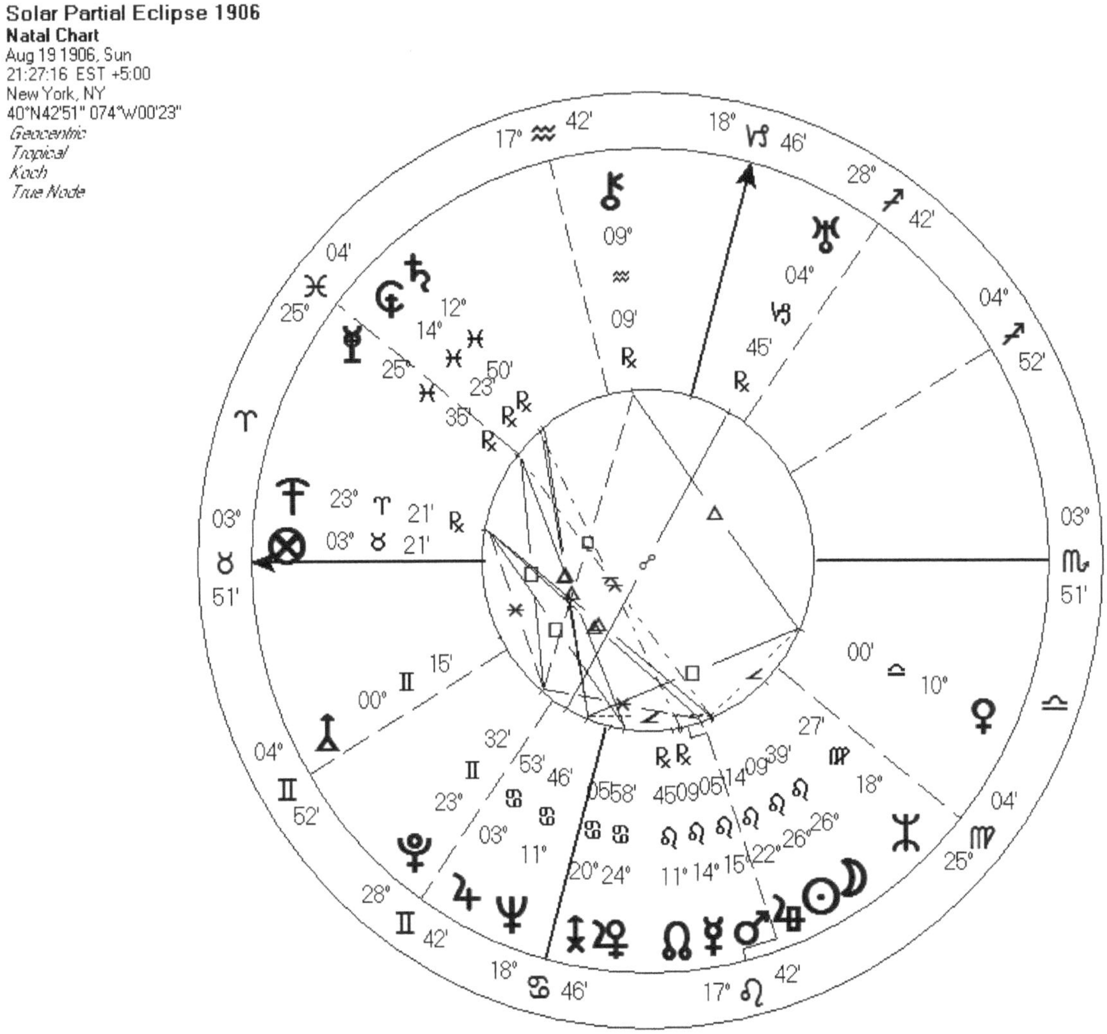

At the time of this third solar eclipse in Saros series 153, the Dow Jones Average of industrial stocks stood at 95.34. Six months later, on February 19, 1907, that index had fallen to 92.28, for a net loss of 3.21 percent.

But that loss was just the tip of the iceberg, with a much greater impact on the stock market still to come during the remainder of 1907. By mid-November, with the Panic of 1907 taking its toll, a look at the Dow Jones Industrial Average showed that that market gauge had lost another 42 percent, closing as low as 53.00 that month.

PARTIAL SOLAR ECLIPSE – AUGUST 30, 1924

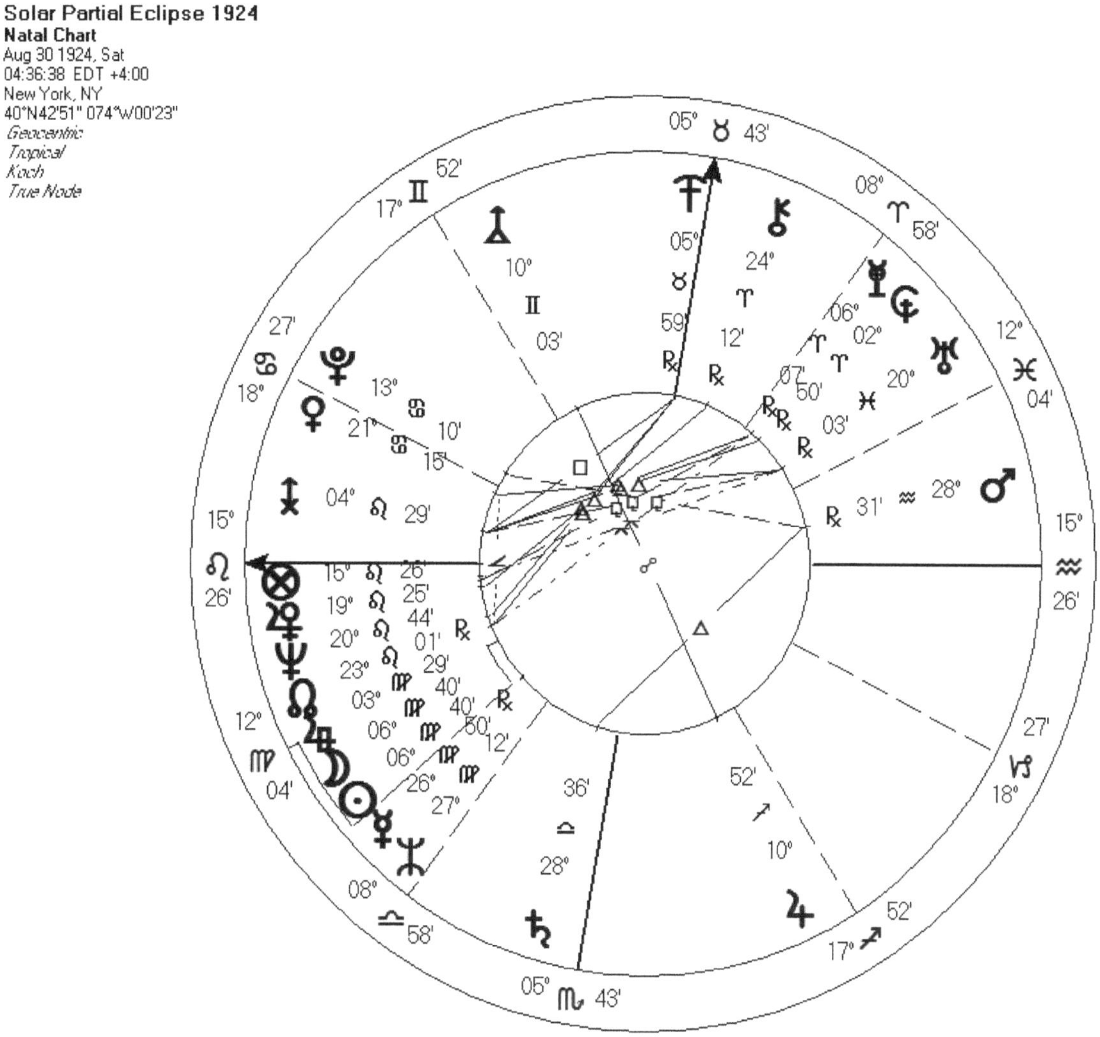

The solar eclipse on August 30, 1924 took place just one week after Mars had made its closest approach to Earth since the tenth centrury, but astrologically Mars was disposited by Saturn, and just separating from a trine with the planet of restrictions. It was a time when some restrictions and new structures were needed.

A big factor in the euphoric delusions of the time was likely the Neptune/Cupido conjunction at the time of the solar eclipse, promoting popular flights of fancy in combination with Poseidon, the transneptunian factor connected with lofty idealism, conjoining Mercury, which was the final dispositor for most of the planetary action in the eclipse horoscope.

Like the initial eclipse in Saros series 153, this solar eclipse also marked a time when efforts were made to avert financial catastrophes. On August 29, the day before the eclipse, Germany adopted the Dawes Plan for financial reform, a scheme which had been developed by a commission headed by Chicago banker Charles Gates Dawes to deal with the runaway inflation that Germany had been experiencing.

Under the terms of the plan, Berlin issued a new Reichsmark, which was backed 30 percent by Gold and which had a value equal to one billion of the old German marks, which had essentially become worthless in the commercial realm. The Dawes Plan also specified that the old German marks would be removed from circulation in a currency recall.

In the U.S., however, there was a strong emphasis on leisure activities rather than on austerity. The Roaring Twenties were very much in play. The Saturday trading session for U.S. Stocks on August 30, 1924 closed at 105.16. Six months later, on March 3, 1925, the stock index closed at 128.26. This was a gain of 17.21 percent.

PARTIAL SOLAR ECLIPSE – SEPTEMBER 10, 1942

The next solar eclipse in Saros series 153 took place as the U.S. was expanding its role in World War II, on September 10, 1942. Nine days earlier, a U.S. Federal Court had upheld the legality of mass internment of Japanese-American citizens in government prison camps, with anti-Japanese and anti-German sentiments both running high.

The day before the eclipse, Japanese planes launched the first attack of the war on continental U.S. Soil, dropping incendiary bombs on Mount Emily, Oregon. On the date of the solar eclipse the British invaded Madagascar and the Royal Air Force dropped more than 100,000 bombs on the German city of Dusseldorf. In the days immediately following the eclipse, the German army broke through Russian defenses and reduced the city of Stalingrad to rubble, and the Japanese initiated a series of deadly assaults in the Battle of Edson's Ridge on the island of Guadalcanal.

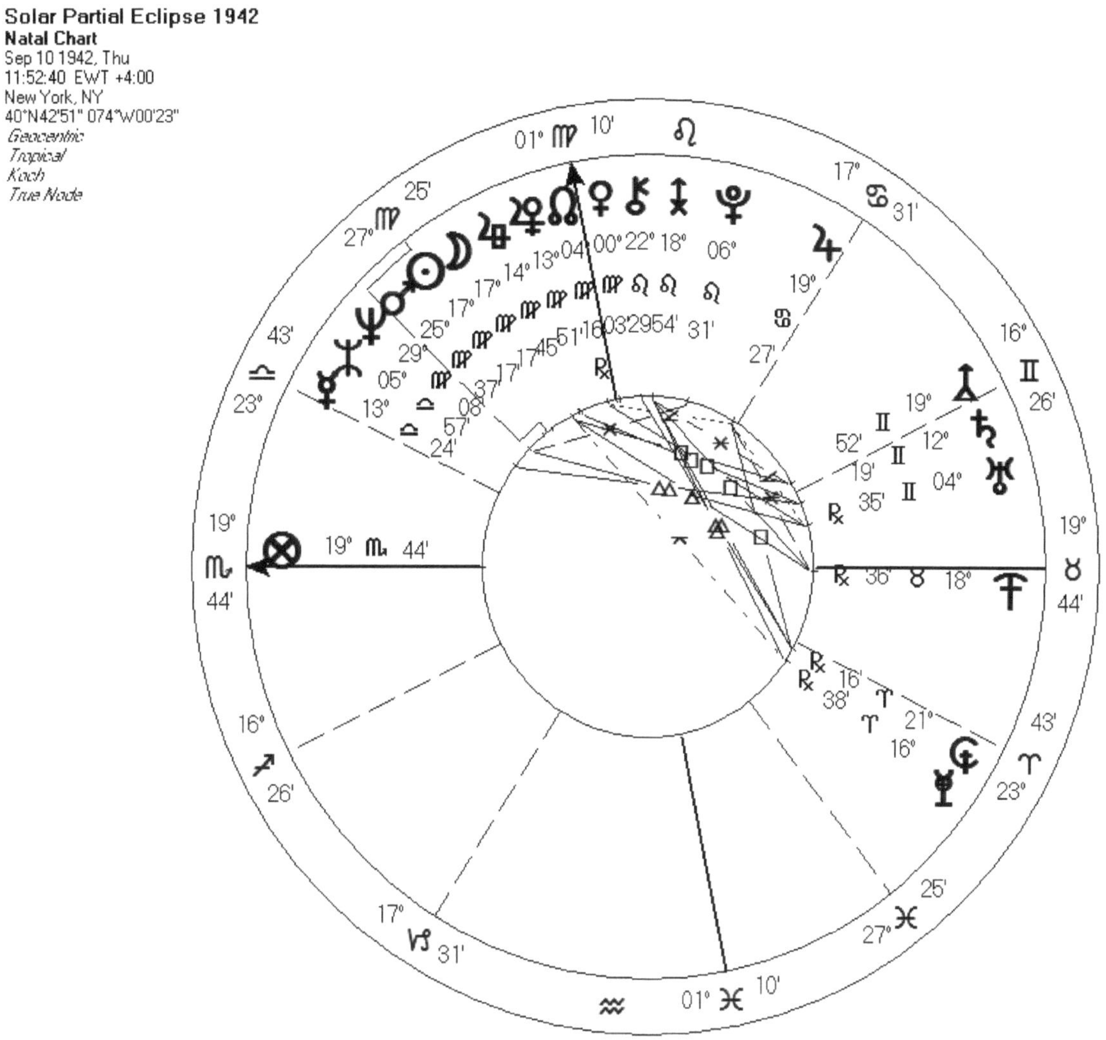

With the expansion of the war, critical materials were brought into the public spotlight. Gasoline was rationed, and on the day of the eclipse the Baruch Commission warned of a potential "military and civilian collapse" due to a shortage of rubber. In general there was also a need for a greater commitment of financial resources to the war effort, requiring substantial growth in government revenues.

The congressional response to that need was the Revenue Act of 1942, legislation which imposed a 5 percent "victory tax" on all annual individual incomes over $624. It was the largest revenue bill in U.S. History, and it was to stay in effect for the remainder of the war years.

But wartime shortages and the added tax burden didn't keep U.S. businesses from doing well. On the date of the September 1942 solar eclipse the Dow Industrials closed at 106.38. Six months later, on March 10, 1943, that index closed at 129.80, with a gain of 22.02 percent.

PARTIAL SOLAR ECLIPSE – SEPTEMBER 20, 1960

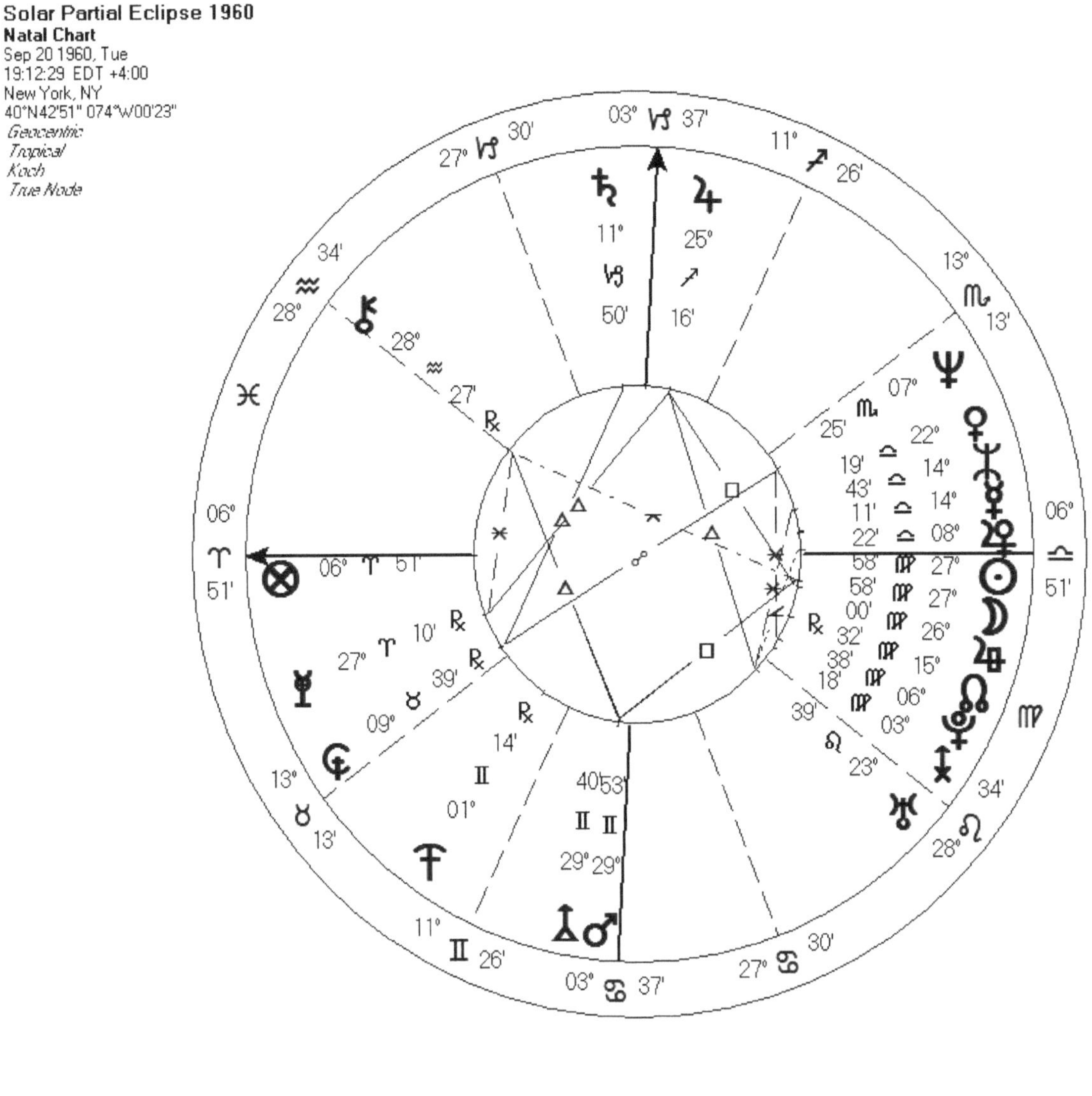

The arrival of the next solar eclipse in Saros series 153, on September 20, 1960, came in the midst of a tumultuous time in the Western hemisphere and elsewhere. In the days just before the eclipse, Cuba nationalized the U.S. banks in that island nation, including First National City Bank of New York, First National Bank of Boston, and Chase Manhattan Bank. Even so, the Cuban leader Fidel Castro was cheered by crowded in the streets of New York City when he arrived there to attend the United Nations General Assembly.

Castro's "brief" speech at the U.N. on September 26 lasted for more than four hours. On the same day, presidential candidates Richard M. Nixon and John F. Kennedy met in Chicago for the first televised presidential debate in history. Meanwhile on the radio, Chubby Checker's "Twist" was enjoying a multi-week run as the number one hit record.

Much of the highly dramatic energy of that time is reflected in the horoscope for the solar eclipse, with an extremely volatile Mars/Vulcanus conjunction square the eclipse point, with the eclipse itself (like the one in October 2014) conjoining the transneptunian factor Apollon. Note as well that Jupiter at the time of the eclipse formed both a square to Apollon and a trine to Uranus, for a further confirmation of the expansionary temper of the time.

These dynamic astrological configurations helped energized the stock market as well – on the date of the solar eclipse in September 1960, the Dow Industrials closed at 588.20; six months later, on March 20, 1961, the index had climbed by 15.41 percent to close at 678.84.

PARTIAL SOLAR ECLIPSE – OCTOBER 2, 1978

Lebanon was a global hot spot in the fall of 1978, and in the days leading up to the solar eclipse on October 2 Syria escated its attacks on Christian militias in Lebanon, with a loss of more than 1,200 Lebanese and 200 Syrian lives. Things settled down briefly a few days after the eclipse when Israel threatened to intervene in the conflict.

In the Western hemisphere, tensions were running high in Guatemala, where a general strike on the day of the solar eclipse paralyzed the country and resulted in more than 1,000 arrests and 30 deaths. Just one week prior to the eclipse one of the worst air disasters in U.S. history occurred when a private plane collided with a Pacific Southwest Airlines 727 jet in the sky over San Diego, California, killing the pilot of the small plane, all 137 people aboard the 727, and an undetermined number of people on the ground when the flaming wreckage plummeted into a residential neighborhood.

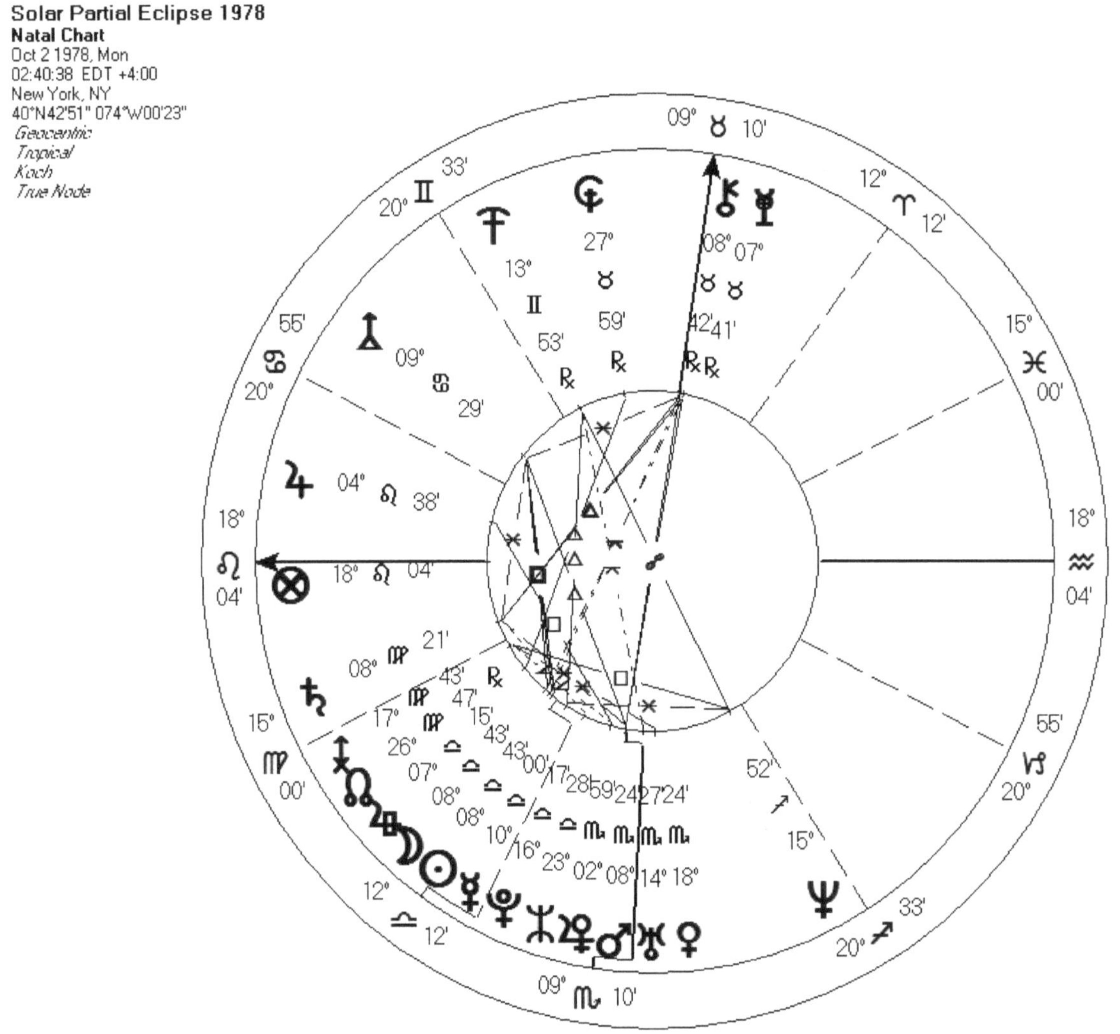

But perhaps the most dramatic event associated with the solar eclipse in October 1978 was the death of Pope John Paul I, the "smiling pope," on September 30, just two days before the eclipse. He had only been elevated to the papacy a month earlier, on August 27, and his death, although reportedly caused by a sudden heart attack, immediately attracted the attention of conspiracy theorists, who suspected that his liberal views had attracted foul play from freemasons or from other forces in a clandestine Vatican power struggle. His successor was named three weeks after the eclipse – John Paul II, the first non-Italian pope in 455 years.

While the horoscope for the October 1978 solar eclipse features the same conjunction of Apollon with the eclipse point that we have seen elsewhere in the eclipses of this Saros series, we can more logically attribute the violence associated with that event to Mars, which is the final dispositor of the eclipse horoscope. It is also the most angular planet in the chart set for New York City, and it's noteworthy because of its opposition to an ominous conjunction of Chiron and Admetos. That Chiron/Admetos combination is extraordinarily powerful, and its "inconveniently limiting" energy is amplified by its trine to Saturn and by its quincunx to the solar eclipse point itself.

That highly restrictive tendency was also reflected in the stock market in the months following this solar eclipse, with much of the trading action confined to a fairly narrow price range. On October 2, 1978, with the close of the markets after the solar eclipse that day, the Dow Industrials stood at 867.90. Six months later, on April 2, 1979, the trading range hadn't changed much – the Dow Industrials closed at 855.25, with a net decline of just 1.46 percent.

PARTIAL SOLAR ECLIPSE – OCTOBER 12, 1996

The most recent solar eclipse in Saros series 153 took place on October 12, 1996. Less than a week before eclipse incumbent U.S. President Bill Clinton met Republican challenger Bob Dole in their first televised debate prior to the November election. On the day after that debate, News Corporation launched the Fox News Channel as a 24/7 competition to CNN. Four days after the solar eclipse, tragedy struck at a soccer stadium in Guatemala when 47,000 football fans tried to squeeze into the 36,000-seat

Estadio Mateo Flores in Guatemala City. The melee left 84 dead and more than 180 injured.

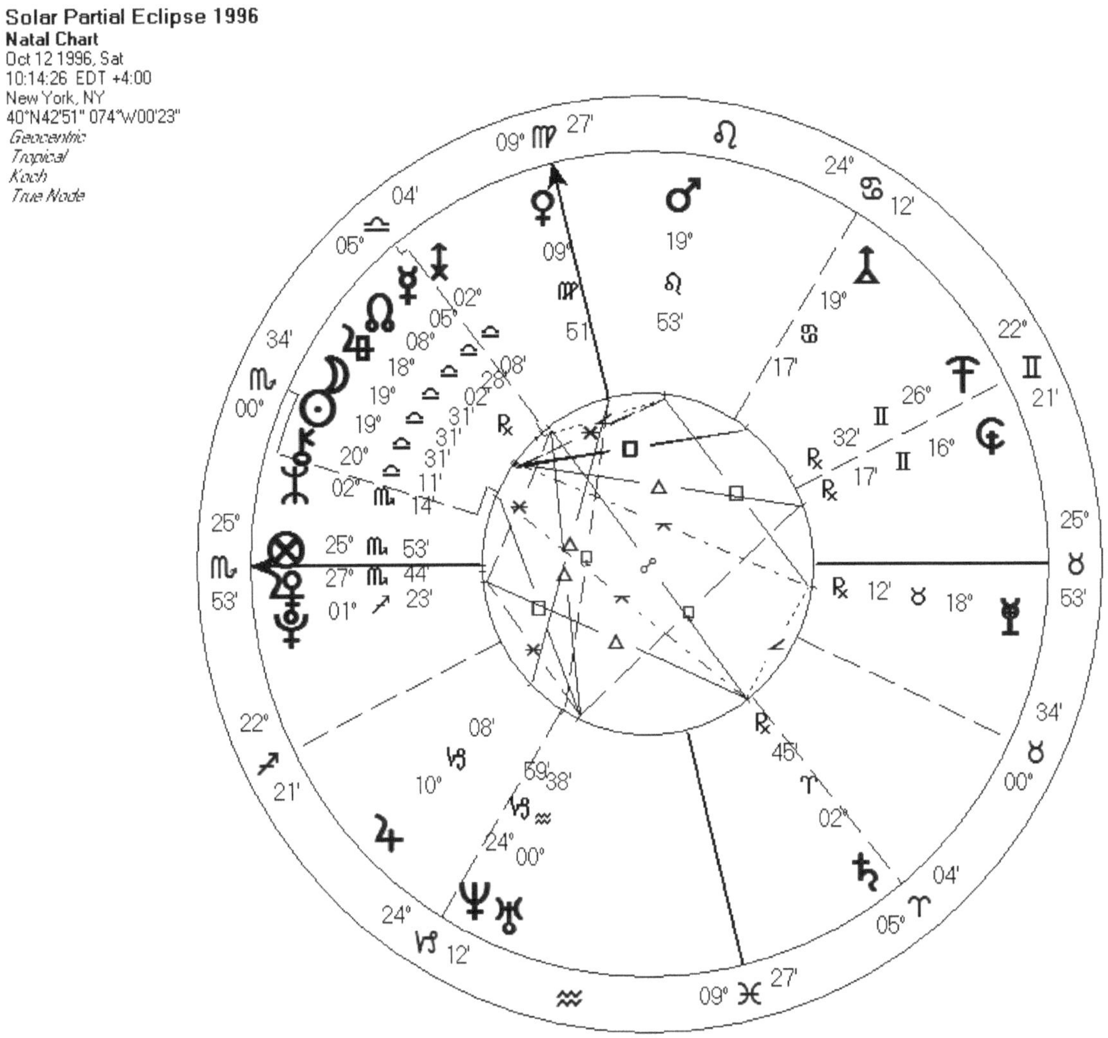

The horoscope for this event repeats the motif of Apollon conjoining the eclipse point, but in this case the configuration is energized by a squre from Vulcanus. Mars has much less potency than we've seen in some of the other horoscopes; even though it's in a sextile to the eclipse point, its energy is inhibited by a square from the restrictive transneptunian Admetos. The most angular planet in the chart is Venus, which, in a mutual reception with Mercury, acts as one of the final dispositors for the horoscope. This suggests a time with a strong focus on discovering and communicating refinements and enhancements in general, and on activities that can improve the overall economic and financial outlook, especially since Venus is applying to a trine with Jupiter.

That positive economic drive became evident almost immediately after the solar eclipse. On October 14, just two days after the event, the Dow Jones Industrial Average closed above the 6,000 mark for the first time in history. On the date of the solar eclipse the Dow stood at 5,969.38, but six months later it was at 6,391.69, representing a net gain in the index of 7.07 percent.

In reviewing all of these previous eclipses in Saros Series 153, we can reach a few interesting conclusions, which may help us understand some of the potential that's built into the solar eclipse of October, 2014.

There seems to be a fairly strong connection between these eclipses and times of economic or financial crisis, from the actions by the Bank of England to raise interest rates in 1870 and the need to boost tax revenues in 1942 to the change in German currency in 1924 and the nationalization of American banks in Cuba in 1960. And while this series of solar eclipses has hardly been exempt from catastrophic events, the typical pattern is one of crisis resolution rather than hopeless consternation.

With half of the solar eclipse points in this series conjoining Apollon, it's not unexpected to see a strong record of market bullishness associated with the events. Stock prices rose during the six-month periods following the solar eclipse in more than 70 percent of the cases, and the overall increase in stock prices in those periods averaged 8.49 percent.

While we can gain a lot from examining the solar eclipses in Saros Series 153 as a precursor to the current solar eclipse, with an eye toward understanding the events we can expect in the future, I think it is also important to observe just how this current eclipse connects with specific geographical areas. When we are tuned in to the various geographical connections, we can be much more alert for potentially profitable trading opportunities, and we can also engage in some creative thinking that may open the door to possibilities that we may not have otherwise considered.

That's why I'm especially pleased to include some comments and perspectives from my colleague Jim Cummins, an accomplished mundane astrologer (and fine musician) who regularly reviews the geopolitical implications and socioeconomic ramifications of cosmic events for our members at FinancialCyclesWeekly.com.

In the next section of this report, you'll find out what Jim has to say about the global ramifications of the solar eclipse of October 2014:

Geopolitical Dynamics of the Solar Eclipse of October 23, 2014

by Jim Cummins

As the illustration on page 19 of this report shows, the Partial Solar Eclipse of 23 October 2014 begins in the North Pacific Ocean, below the center tip of Russia's Kamchatka Peninsula, heading on a northeastward arc through the Shelekhov Gulf; across the Siberian province of Chukotskiy to enter the East Siberian Sea above the Arctic Circle; then across the top the world over the Arctic Ocean before gently turning landward to reach its greatest eclipse point in Canada's Nunavut Territory near Prince of Wales Island, on a trajectory that takes it over the western sector of the Hudson Bay; through Ontario; to enter the United States near where Lake Michigan and Lake Huron come together.

Its path of totality (approx. 70 miles wide) continues down through Michigan; over Ft. Wayne, Indiana; Louisville, Kentucky; Murfreesboro, Tennessee; and Ft. Payne, Alabama to enter the Gulf of Mexico from near Fort Walton Beach, Florida; passing just to the east of the northernmost tip of the Yucatan Peninsula; and culminating a few miles north of Honduras, in the Caribbean Sea.

This Eclipse is visible, and its effects will be felt all over Japan; across far eastern Siberia; the Arctic Ocean; and throughout the North American continent, plus Mexico and Central America, except for the far eastern side of Canada, and the upper north-eastern states in the United States.

The greatest impact of a solar eclipse's effects always follow closely its approximately 70-mile wide path of totality (generally described above), and fan out from there in a broad semi-circular arc between the beginning and ending points of the eclipse shadow. However there is a corresponding decrease in the potency of its effects in direct ratio to the distance one is from the path of totality.

Every geographical area that is highlighted, and caught within the eclipse path's "net", will be subject to this eclipse's impact. This is especially so in this particular case, because of the geological sensitivity of all these areas. Weather extremes, geological and seismic disturbances of all manner, will attend this eclipse throughout its duration, and across every area and location from which it will have been visible, especially in those areas already prone to such geological or seismic disturbances.

These will be an on-going set of continuous conditions. Please be prepared, and ever alert. Also please keep visiting Tim Bost's Financial Cycles Weekly (www.financialcyclesweekly.com) regularly and go to the *Big Picture Perspectives* section for the updates I'll be providing pertaining to potential dates and locations for events relating to this Solar Eclipse (October 23, 2014).

The duration for the effects of this eclipse is at least six months. That may extend to a year or more, because of the trajectory of the next Solar Eclipse, which will take place on March 20, 2015, and also traverse the Arctic Ocean.

As the October 23, 2014 Solar Eclipse spotlights North America, especially the United States, from the Arctic Ocean, the March 20, 2015 Solar Eclipse will cast its broad "net" all across Europe and Euro-Asia, also from the Arctic Ocean.

Considering that the Solar Eclipse of April 29, 2014 shadowed Antarctica, and the following two Solar Eclipses are shadowing the Arctic Ocean, the obvious pattern places tremendous emphasis on the Polar regions of the Earth. This has huge significance, which will be discussed in upcoming *Big Picture Perspectives* articles, to be published on the Financial Cycles Weekly site (www.financialcyclesweekly.com).

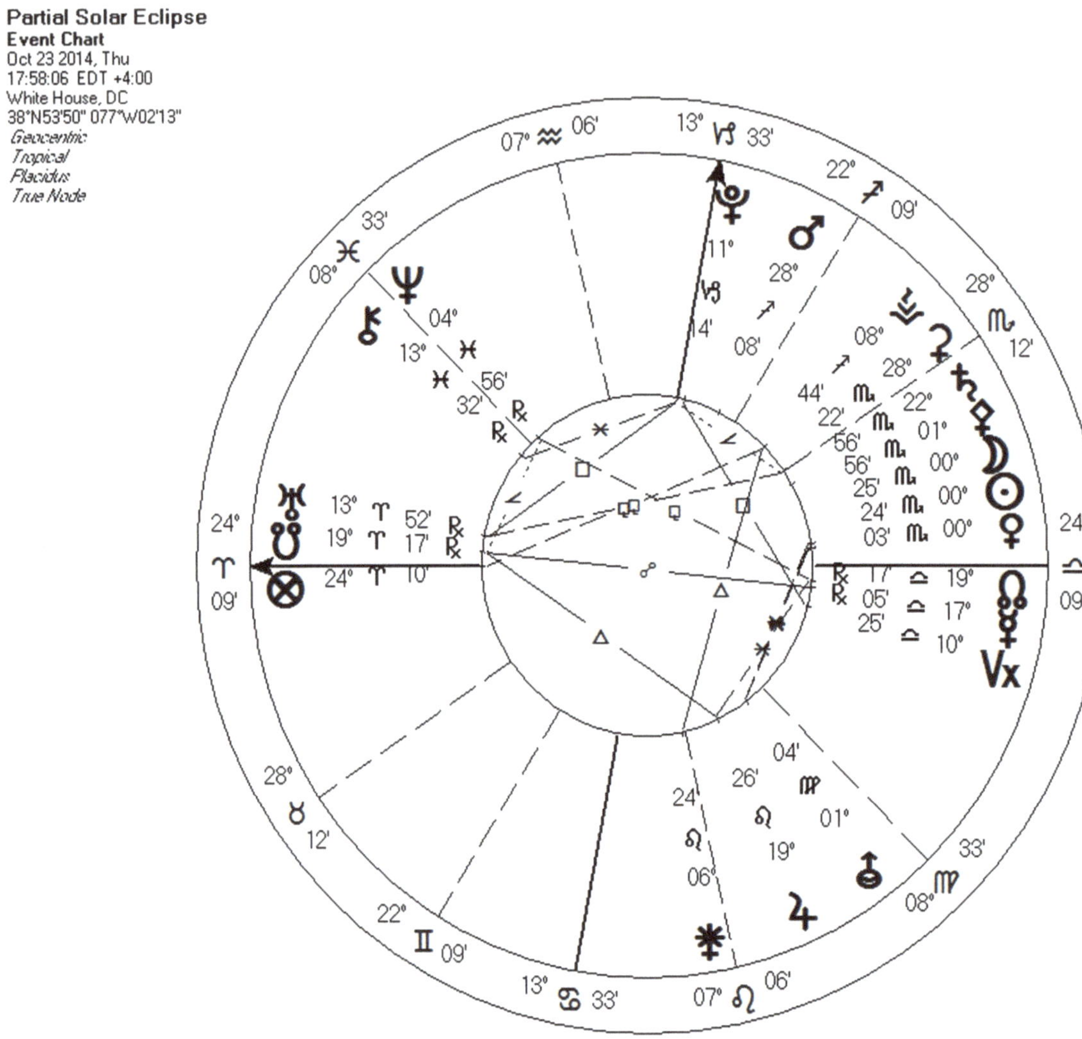

This is the Natal Chart for the Partial Solar Eclipse of October 23, 2014, as seen from the White House, in Washington, D.C.

At first glance, this chart seems rather benign, with Venus being conjunct the eclipse point, as well as that planet being the dispositor of the Vertex, Mercury (Retrograde, but about to turn Stationary Direct), and the North Node, which are all in Libra, immediately preceding the eclipse.

This eclipse enjoys a separating Sextile to Mars, and an applying Trine to Neptune. In and of themselves, these are traditionally very favorable alignments.

The prevailing Uranus square Pluto *(you'd think we'd all be used to this revolutionary, transformative aspect by now!)* is akin to a charged electrical wire without an insulating sheath. This characteristic obtains even with Uranus being Retrograde, in the 12th House, and seemingly backing away from the South Node, which it will later conjunct (1 Feb. 2015), once Uranus has turned Direct (22 Dec. 2014) and the two close towards one another.

The Ascendant/Descendant axis in this chart is closely aligned with the Lunar Eclipse degree of 15 April 2014, which added to the intensities of the Ukrainian crisis at that time. That issue is nowhere near settled, nor will it be in the foreseeable future – until Vladimir Putin has completely returned Ukraine to the Russian fold. It will continue to flare up in the months to come.

This Solar Eclipse takes place at 0 degrees of Scorpio. Scorpio is a Fixed Sign. Being "Fixed" is like being single-minded, with a fixidity or definiteness of purpose, sometimes seemingly slow, but always steady and persistent.

Scorpio is the most intense of all the Signs. It represents things that belong to others, but which accrue to the individual (or entity) represented by the chart – i.e., OPM, (other people's money), legacies, inheritances, etc. and the benefits derived by the absorption of those shared, or inherited values. Therefore, it signifies the banking and insurance industries, et al; investments and anything that can enhance the owner of the chart as a result of the efforts and volition of others..

This Solar Eclipse, as viewed from the White House in Washington, D. C., falls into the 7th House – the House of Open Enemies or Partnerships. Although Venus is very present in conjunction to this eclipse point, (*Venus also represents money, among other things of beauty and value*), this Venus is the Libran-natured Venus, being the dispositor of both Mercury (Retrograde) and the North Node, each of which is in Libra.

Therefore, this Venus symbolizes *NEGOTIATIONS and AGREEMENTS* established by and between moneyed interests – and since we are dealing with a Scorpio eclipse, this signifies *very powerful moneyed interests*…especially monies which can be taxed, or which bear interest, and/or which can be hidden or maneuvered, and subject to sabatoge by clever, disguised manipulations.

The Solar Eclipse of this chart identifies the type of persons, firms, corporations, NGO's, and state entities who engage in such activities – shrewd, callous, very secretive, often very ambitious and treacherous entities.

This Eclipse chart attests to powerful interests, including the BRICS nations and all their allies, the IMF and BIS, etc., who are dedicated to undermining, and ultimately destroying the U.S. Dollar as the world's Reserve Currency. It also shows that they are now extremely close to achieving that objective.

There is a huge *financial war* presently underway in the halls of economic powers between those who might loosely be termed the Asian Illuminati vs. the Western Democracies' Illuminati. America's Federal Reserve System, as well as most, if not all of the world's Central Banks, will ultimately become morphed into which ever system 'wins' that war. This *financial war* will have been won, and the 'New Global Economic Order" will be in place by 2025, if not before. That is when all the outer planets form an enduring (several years in succession) period of peaceful, cooperative Trines and Sextiles one to another.

Wherever an eclipse falls in relation to the natal charts of prominent personalities, or those who hold the reins of authority in various settings, whether on a small scale or large, describes how that eclipse affects those personalities, and through them, whomever is accountable to, or subject to, those individuals.

In this particular situation: Here is the Natal Chart of the United States of America (center circle) with the October 23, 2014 Solar Eclipse planet placements around it in the outer circle:

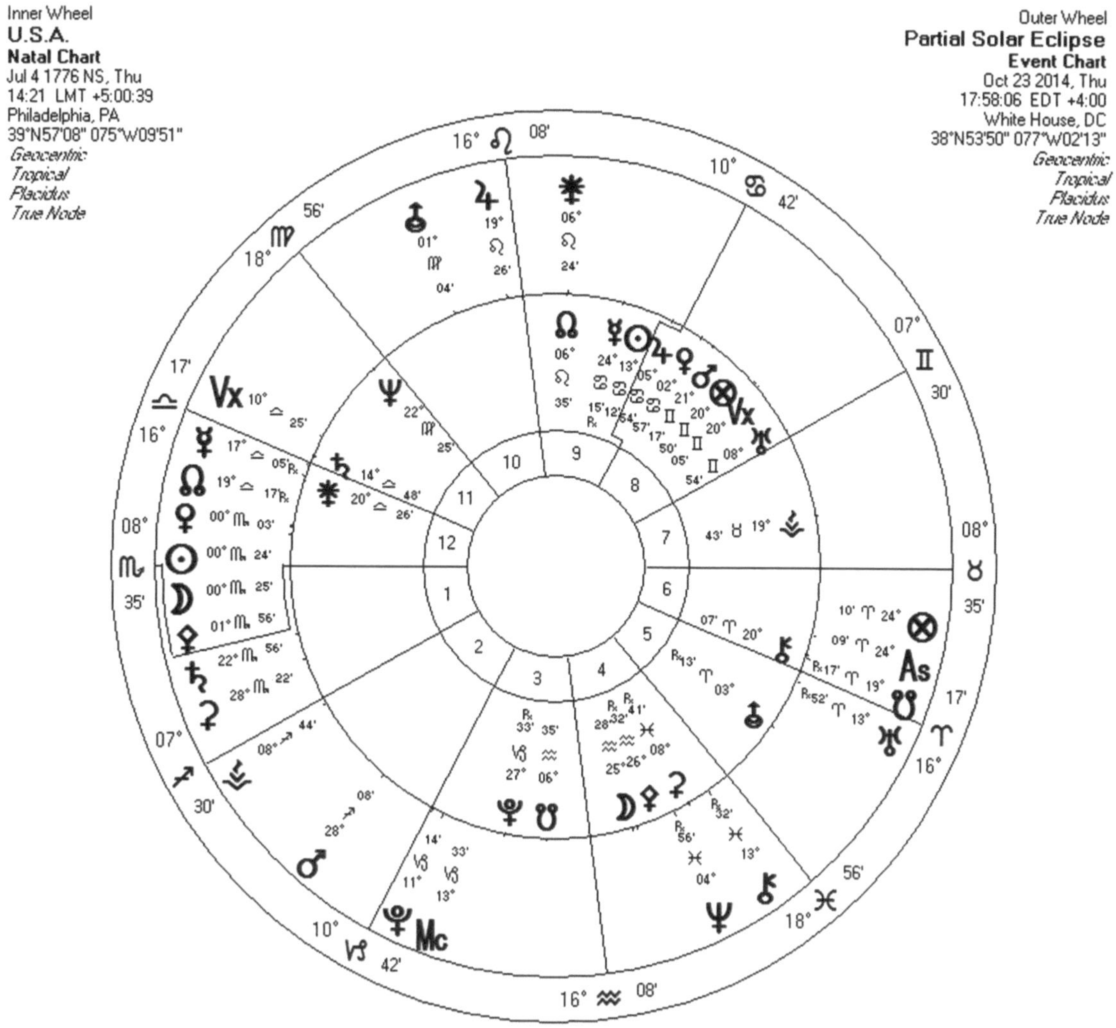

This Solar Eclipse falls into the 12th House of America's Natal Chart. In a Mundane wheel, the 12th House corresponds to disturbances or conditions that work against the public welfare. The 12th House rules correctional institutions, places of detention, jails, prisons, and all places of confinement, such as hospitals, retirement homes, etc. It rules things that are hidden; secret groups, secret government entities, spies and secret enemies. It rules crime and criminals, *terrorist activities*, hostage situations, behind the scenes manipulations, involuntary services ordered by law, organizations devoted to forcible control or condemnation of people, slavery, covert aggression and conditions of exile.

[NOTE: This eclipse announces a significantly heightened period of potential for terrorist activities within the American Homeland. Please refer to Tim Bost's Financial Cycles Weekly (www.financalcyclesweekly.com), in upcoming Big Picture Perspectives articles for more detailed information regarding these matters.]

In other words, the 12th House, in a Mundane (political) chart is a tough place to be, and an especially tough place into which a Solar Eclipse might fall.

In its own nativity, as viewed from the White House, this Solar Eclipse degree naturally falls into the 7th House of Open Enemies and/or Partners.

But, when paired with the Natal Chart of the USA, this Solar Eclipse falls into the USA's12th House of Hidden Enemies, indicating that those opponents and/or adversaries who otherwise would be readily recognized, so they could be dealt with appropriately, become obscured, hidden from view, and not at all obvious as enemies or opponents or adversaries, regardless their appearance or intent.

The 12th House placement for this Solar Eclipse shows that those powerful enemies, both foreign and domestic, are very present among us, developing and executing their nefarious schemes against us.

There is nonetheless a relatively bright side to this overlay: The natural Trine in the Solar Eclipse chart between the Solar Eclipse and its Neptune fits beautifully into a Grand Trine configuration with America's Natal Venus and Jupiter in USA's 8th House. Furthermore, when we note that the proximity of America's Natal Moon and Pallas are within orb of a Trine to the Solar Eclipse degree, the "Green Zone" of the Grand Trine between the two charts is considerably widened, and therefore holds much more potential for beneficial behind-the-scenes *NEGOTIATIONS and AGREEMENTS*, during the tenure of this Solar Eclipse –which will be active for at least the next six (6) months.

Several other favorable alignments support this opportune advantage.. Among them is Solar Eclipse's Jupiter, sitting prominently in America's 10th

House of Honors, Recognition, Applause, and all the things which signify public approval and individual achievement. That SE Jupiter is extremely well- aspected in the Solar Eclipse chart, with a Sextile to the SE Moon's North Node (which itself conjuncts SE Mercury Retrograde), and a Trine to the SE South Node, while simultaneously Sextiling America's Natal Vertex-Pars Fortuna-Mars triple conjunction in the USA 8th House of benefit through the support of others.

All these factors are absolutely SUPERB indicators of the potential for an enduring period of very successful, behind-the-scenes *negotiations, and agreements,* specifically updated trade agreements with our neighbors to the South, i.e., Mexico, Latin and South America.

Most importantly, however, is just who's side will this Administration be on when it comes to solidifying agreements with Iran?

The SE Mercury, Retrograde, but about to Station Direct, is conjunct America's Natal Saturn. America has only two (2) natural Squares in her Natal Chart; her Sun square her Saturn; and her Mars square her Neptune.

Mercury conjunct Saturn, in and of itself, represents 'profundity of thought'. These two planets, when unobstructed, can work extremely well together. This conjunction is often found in the charts of brilliant scientists, authors, engineers, etc.

However, Mercury is Retrograde here....leaving much UNsaid that should be said – allowing details to be missed, or overlooked – deliberately or unintentionally. Our (America's) Natal Saturn being square to her Sun shows just how important the details and specifics in contracts, and contractual relationships are, and especially how vital it is that they be constructed within the framework (Saturn) of all applicable laws (9th House – Law; 11th House – corporate or big-business undertakings). The 11th House in a Mundane chart also represents the Congress, the Law-making branch of our government.

The several Trines and Sextiles already mentioned indicate that this Solar Eclipse signifies that the time is ripe for highly successful, mutually beneficial *NEGOTIATIONS and AGREEMENTS.*

Issues involving American and Canadian interests vs. Russian claims, etc., will certainly take on magnified significance during the course of this eclipse's tenure.

Having a steady, and patriotic hand at the helm of negotiations concerning these matters will be of primary concern for all Americans.

The inherent square between America's Natal Sun and her Saturn, activated by the SE Mercury, shows that even though the energies and opportunities for successful negotiations are certainly present, the 'devil is in the details' so to speak, and hammering out the specifics will not only be challenging, but could be sabatoged with deliberately included obfuscations, and ambiguities.

Even so, – this is nonetheless an excellent period for significant 'breakthroughs', on numerous fronts. This eclipse can be like a ray of sunlight after a long, stormy night. Those in positions of authority would do well to take full advantage of it.

This very special Solar Eclipse *(there will not be another to so definitively highlighting America until August, 2017*) turns the world's spotlight on America.

What we say and do as a Nation is being watched very closely now – and will be so between now and next Spring (2015). We, the USA, have an exceptional opportunity to regain at least some of the International Good Will that America once enjoyed, if only we are able to *negotiate and complete* the kinds of *agreements* that can be universally recognized for being as beneficial for our adversaries and/or opponents as they are for us.

That is the potential symbolized in this very powerful Solar Eclipse, when considered in context with America's Natal Chart.

See on the next page President Barack Obama's Natal Chart:.

(Caveat: *No one knows for absolute certainty Barack Obama's true birth time and place. He has gone to extreme lengths and enormous expenses to hide that information from the entire world – even to the point of issuing documents that have been proven to be computer created. However, with considerable back-testing, this one seems to be as close to an accurate natal chart for him as this astrologer has so far been able to procure.*)

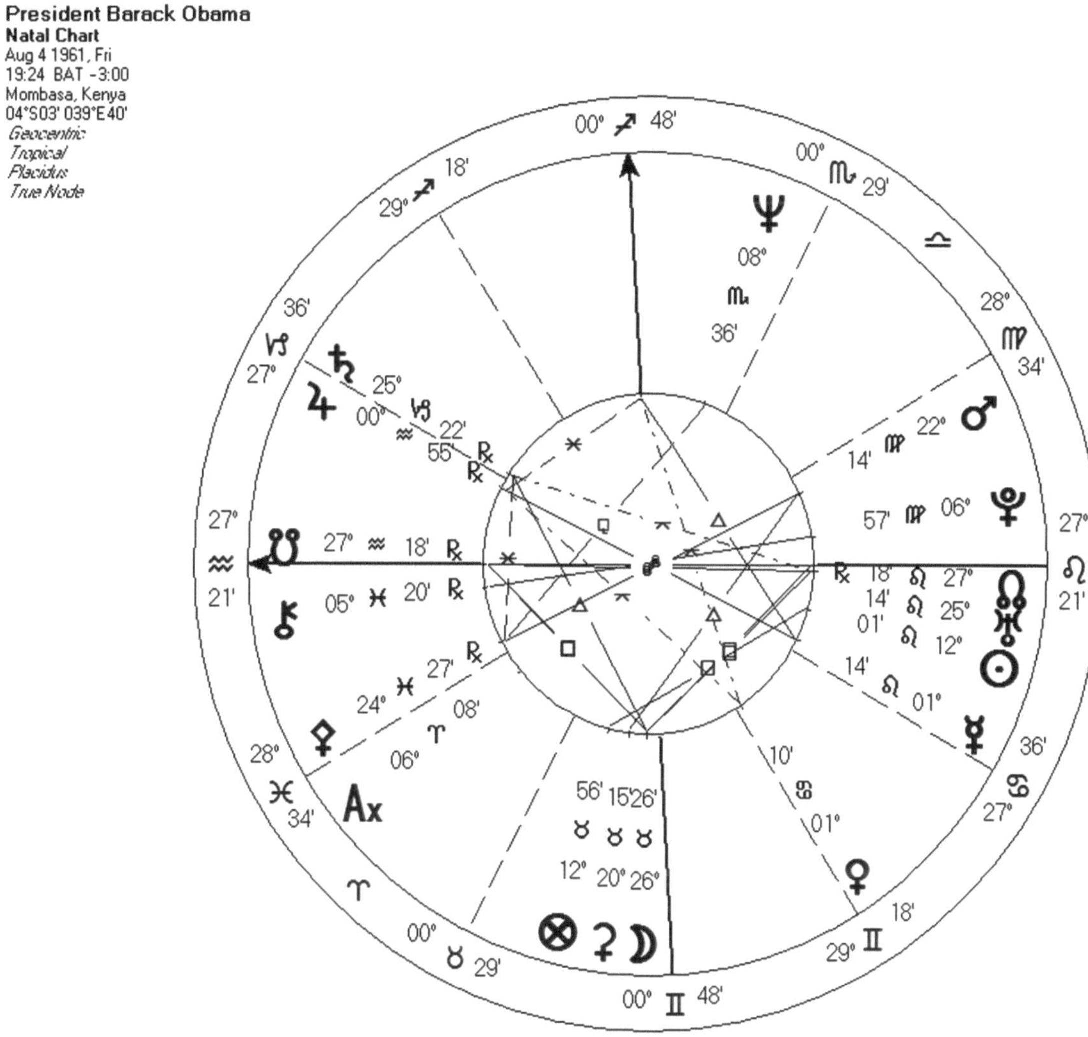

The following bi-wheel chart shows America in the center circle, with President Obama's natal planets around it in the outer circle. The angles between the two sets of planets describe the various ways in which each sees and interacts with the other: i.e., how President Obama sees and interacts with America, and how America sees and interacts with President Obama.

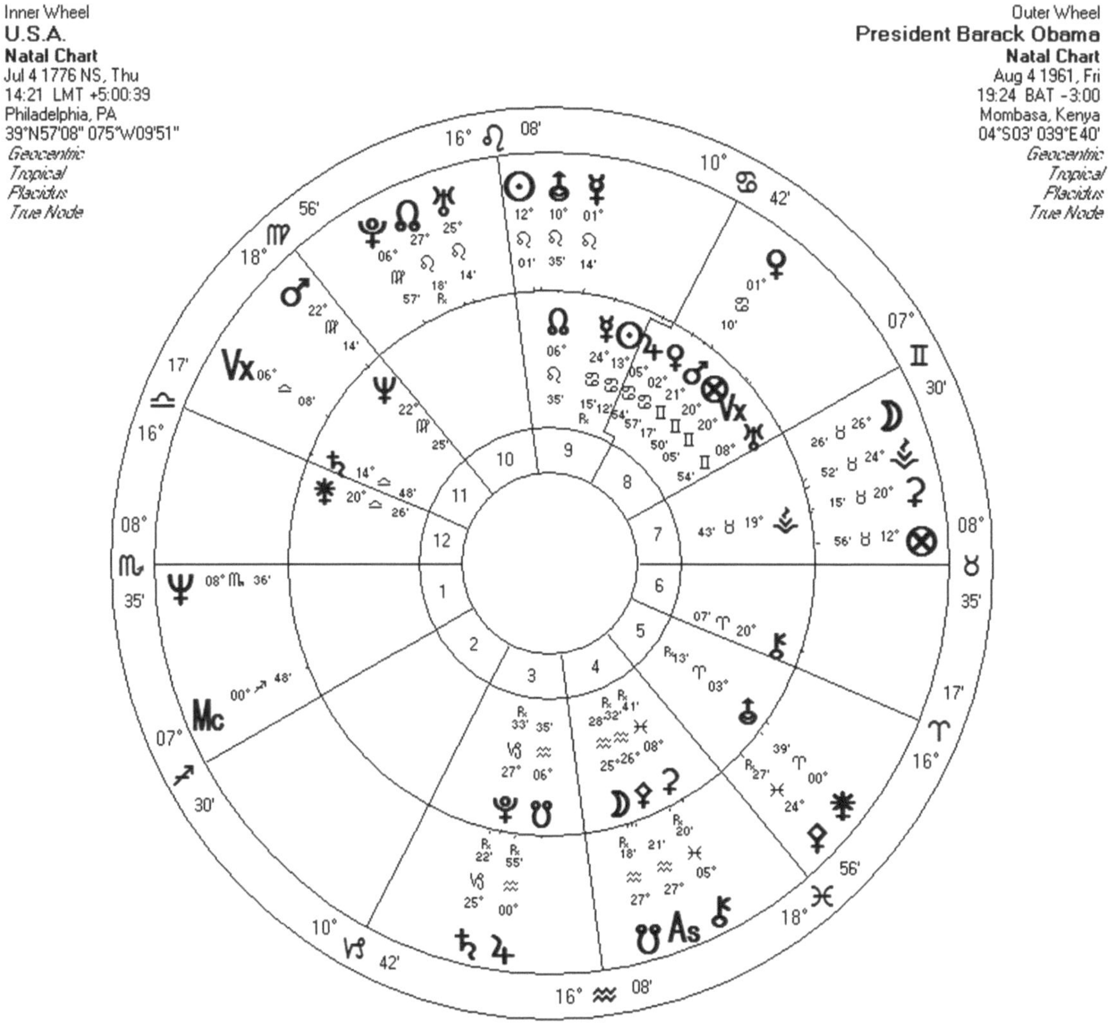

Earlier, I noted that in America's Natal Chart, there are two (2) significant Squares. I wrote of the USA Sun degree being in square aspect to the USA Saturn degree. That's one.

The other square in our National Nativity, is between America's Mars and her Natal Neptune. It is not my purpose here to go into detail defining the many alignments between these charts, but for those of our readers who may not have seen this overlay elsewhere, I will only point out here that Mr. Obama's Natal Neptune is, to the degree, and within only one minute, exactly conjunct America's Ascendant – one of the numerous indicators of his charismatic sway over the vast majority of the populace when he first came onto the scene.

Another alignment that bears close scrutiny is his Natal Mars being conjunct America's Natal Neptune, and therefore square our National Mars. Mars is energy applied…and this configuration indicates that President Obama, by nature, instinctively goes in a direction that is, has always been, and shall always be consistently *at cross purposes* (square) to the direction that America, as a Nation, would choose to go, given a choice in the matter. This is in nearly every undertaking, large or small.

Because Neptune figures prominently in these configuration, it is small wonder that America has made every effort to give him maximum consideration and excessive benefit-of-the-doubt on every issue.

However, as Bob Dylan exclaimed, "*The times, they are a'changin'*", and America is beginning to see things in a clearer light, than they did when transiting Neptune was conjunct their collective National Moon, in late Aquarius (it is now in early Pisces).

President Obama's Natal Saturn and Natal Jupiter straddle America's Natal Pluto (one's Psyche – at the deepest, most transformative level possible), and when we note that the October 23 Solar Eclipse at 0 degrees Scorpio squares President Obama's Natal Jupiter (one's personal "Santa Claus", so to speak – his 'good luck charm'..), it is evident that America is no longer messmerized or transfixed by Barack Obama.

Of greater import, and certainly of concern for President Obama as an individual human being, is the prevailing, transiting Uranus – Pluto square which is the signature of countless social upheavals throughout the world during recent years.

Presently, Uranus is at 13 degrees Aries and Pluto is at 11 degrees Capricorn respectively. Approximately 135 degrees from each of these planets, is 26-28 degrees of Leo. That aspect (angle) is termed a Sesqui-quadrate.

The Sesquiquadrate in the astrological language means, among other things, a "Release of Tension"...much like a fireman's hose sending all the high-pressured water out through a small opening in the nozzle. It releases tension, yes, but must be handled very carefully.

President Obama' Natal Uranus is at 25 degrees Leo, and his Natal North Node is at 27 degrees Leo. Because these two positions conjunct his Natal 7th House, the House of Open Enemies, as well as equitable partnerships, this position, by degree, sign and house, receives from the public the full focus of all that Uranus-Pluto square energy – as a "Release of Tension."

He has already enjoyed this focus quite a lot – in its favorable way. He has been absolutely adored, and put on a pedestal – as long as transiting Neptune covered the same degrees (25-28) in the OPPOSITE Sign of Aquarius – where America's Moon position is – but now (1) transiting Neptune has moved into Pisces, and will not return to Aquarius again for another 148 YEARS....and (2) the October 23, 2014 Solar Eclipse degree Squares his Natal Jupiter, which is in his 12th House, taking much of the luster off that Natal Jupiter, as far as the general public is concerned, while, on the other hand, simultaneously causing him to "double-down' in his untiring efforts to complete his fateful campaign pledge, to ***"Fundamentally transform the United States of America."***

Because the Solar Eclipse energies are *so favorable for negotiations and agreements* over the next several months, and because this Solar Eclipse squares President Obama's Natal Jupiter (among other things), rendering him all the more determined to do whatever he can to implement his original intent vis-à-vis the United States of America, it is highly likely that he will indeed, either directly, or indirectly through subbordinates, make every conceivable concession in giving our adversaries whatever they ask, perhaps hoping that he will be hailed and honored for having procured their agreements.

Sadly, it is more likely that such concessions will be made because his loyalties lie elsewhere than with America.

Stealthily, adroitly, and with renewed vigor and speed, over these next several months especially, President Obama will intensify and redouble his efforts, both overt and covert, to **“fundamentally transform**” the Nation that has given him so much, into the one-party, pared down, submissive, humbled, third-rate Socialistic nation he seems to want America to be.

Consequently, we can expect lots of new, unannounced but sweeping Executive Orders over the next several months.

The October 23, 2014 Solar Eclipse, as viewed from the White House, indicates that America is clearly in danger, from adversaries both outside and inside its walls, boundaries, and borders.

Speaking of boundaries and borders....oh, we won’t go there here!

That is a Saturn and Neptune issue, astrologically speaking. Both of those planets in America’s Natal Chart, are squared, i.e., challenged.

This has always been the case, because it is part of our National Chart. Heretofore, America has always been protected by, and very protective of, her boundaries and borders.

Heretofore, however, America has never had a Commander-in-Chief whose natal planets obstruct the constructive side of those particular configurations in America’s chart.

But now we do.

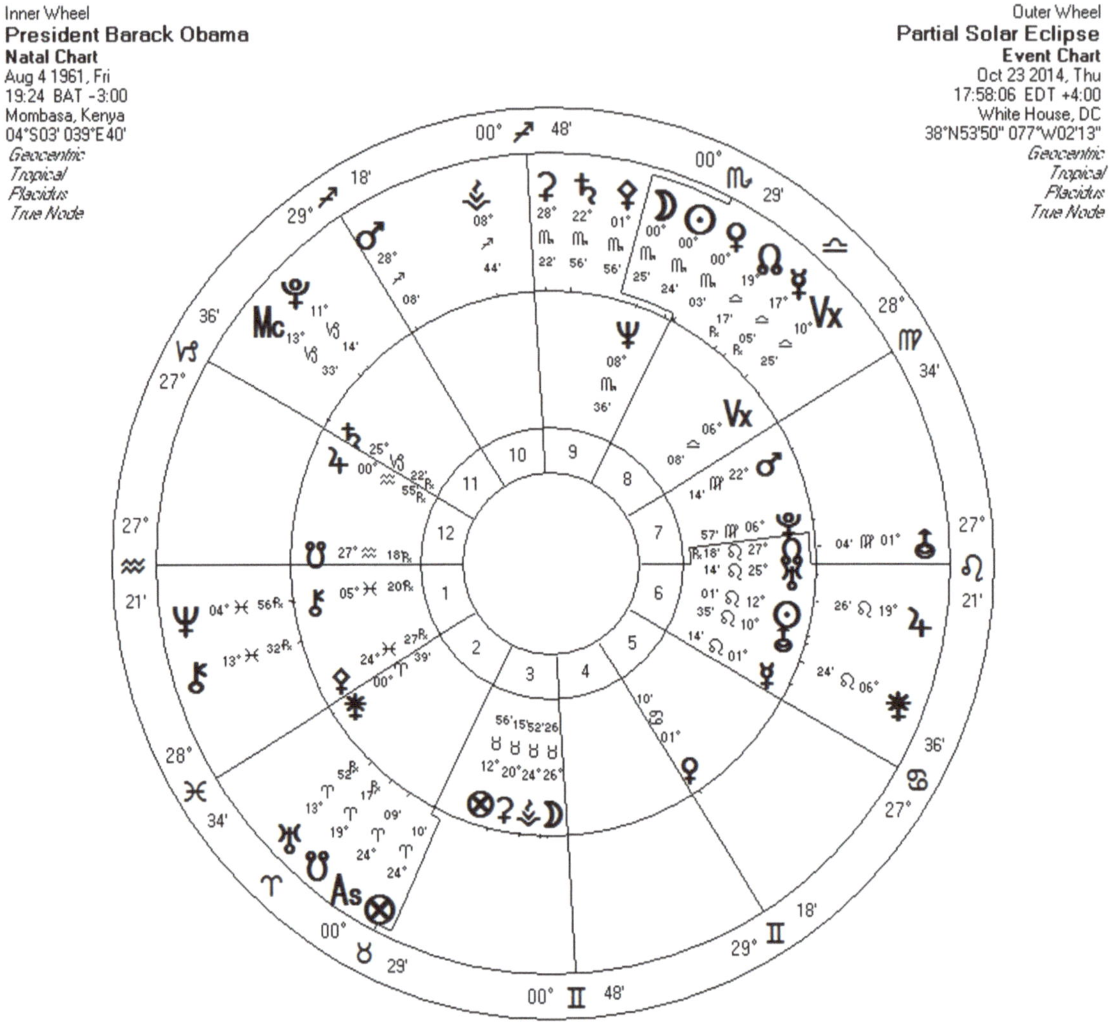

In the overlay between the U.S. Natal Chart and the Solar Eclipse (see page 45), the Solar Eclipse South Node aligns with America's Natal Chiron in her 6th House. In Mundane astrology, the 6th House corresponds to the laboring classes, including Police and Civil Services.

This House rules employment, unemployment, and wage conditions. It rules labor unions and organizations, all branches of the Military, including the Army, Navy, Coast Guard, Air Force, Special Forces; volunteers and organizations that serve in times of crisis, such as First Responders, Fire Fighters, the Red Cross and Salvation Army.

This House also represents public health and health workers, medical services; nursing, dentistry, practioners and healers. Through its connection with health, this House also rules food and drink.

With the Solar Eclipse's South Node transiting this House, and conjuncting America's Natal Chiron there, this area, and all it represents will receive heightened attention during the next 6 months.

America has long shouldered the burden of protecting commerce around the world, by keeping the world's oceans and its sea gates safe for international passage.

It's either commerce, or conflict. No other country could, or would protect the world's flow of goods on the high seas, without either claiming those vital gates and waterways for themselves, and/or exacting a high price on anyone who dared traverse them.

China is a good case in point. Not only is China exerting its hegemony over the South China Sea, and the East China Sea, and thereby challenge of all her neighbors, among other vital waterways, China also already controls both ends to the new Panama Canal.

It doesn't take much imagination to expect that nation to adopt at the Panama Canal the same militant posture she is asserting in the vast South and East China Seas…blocking access and regress of the world's largest tankers, and anyone else who seeks to move goods from one side of the earth to the other without having to go all the way around the bottom of South America.

Whose Navy will challenge China then, to guarantee that one of the world's most vital sea gates remains open and accessible to sea-going traffic from everywhere on Earth?

America has never behaved in such a manner on the world's waterways. We have always protected the universal principle of Freedom of the Seas; and defended the sovereign rights of any and every nation to use and enjoy unimpeded flow of goods and services through the world's oceans and seas.

And we have never exacted a price for that protection, or laid claim to any of those waterways and/or vital sea gates.

But to maintain such a globally significant posture has required that America field the strongest, most flexible Navy the world has ever known – with the assistance of each of the other branches of our exceptional Military.

But in his strange version of what America's Military ought to be, President Obama has nearly decimated that Military at its core, and left it barely able to meet its responsibilities around the world,

(A) by firing more than 260 of America's top Generals (those who he thought might disagree with him and/or his 'lead from behind' policies; and

(B) by instituting the "Sequester" throughout the Armed Forces, causing every branch to enact excessively deep cuts in both personnel and equipment; and

(C) by 'cleansing' and "purging' the training manuals of each of the Branches of Service of any and all words and/or phrases that might conceivably 'offend' any Muslim anywhere.

Soon there will be a showdown in the Arctic, over the vast treasures there. Iceland, Norway, Denmark, Russia, Canada and the United States all have holdings there; some of those territorial holdings are in dispute among them. Now China wants in as well, and is negotiating with Russia for access.

At Universitetskaya, a 7,700-foot well in the Kara Sea, ExxonMobil and their, Russian partner, Rosneft, recently discovered a find which they believe holds about 9 billion barrels of oil. However, this find is already causing tension with the US government, which slapped new sanctions on Russia in the late summer, forbidding US companies from participating in Russian Arctic drilling.

So, according to Kirill Molodtsov, Russia's deputy energy minister, ExxonMobil, who refused to say anything about the discovery, or the 'cease and desist' style order from the US government, drilling will come to a halt on October 10, and the cementing, plugging, and abandoning the well is to be finished by October 18.

This October 23, 2014 Solar Eclipse is the first in a series of eclipses which bring the world's attention to the Arctic Ocean, and its treasures, and disputes, etc. The next Solar Eclipse, on March 20, 2015 will also cast its path of totality over the Arctic Ocean, with its shadow covering nearly all of Europe and EuroAsia.

Between now and then, getting America's house in order is the order of the day, especially for Americans. But American 'house-cleaning' is good for the rest of the world as well. This present (Oct. 23, 2014) Solar Eclipse spotlights America, and it's about time some light came through the window, to wake America up, before it's too late.

When America is strong, safe and secure, the world is strong, safe and secure. We have been weakened – more from within than without. If it takes something as powerful a Solar Eclipse to stir this great and noble Nation from its slumber, then so be it! Good Morning, WORLD!!!!

The Solar Eclipse and Key Financial Horoscopes

While an examination of the horoscope for the October 23 solar eclipse is useful in itself, and while it's extremely helpful to have Jim Cummins' opinions and insights into the geopolitical events that have the potential to move the markets in significant ways, it's also revealing to look at the planets at the time of the eclipse in connection with other important horoscopes – not only those of nations, but also key financial charts.

More and more, however, the financial charts that have been the conventional domain of market astrology are becoming subordinated to national and multi-national charts, as the macroeconomic power of countries, NGO's, and corporations increasingly controls the vital issues that ultimately drive the markets.

Even so, by looking at a selection of key financial horoscopes, we can get a good feel for the economic and investment environment that lies ahead. In each case, we have chosen to show these charts on a 90-degree dial, with the pointer on the dial indicating the position of the October solar eclipse.

Instead of digging into an in-depth analysis of each financial entity, this approach allows us to spot the key midpoint structures that are being activated by the solar eclipse, revealing important dynamics that we might otherwise overlook.

In essence, we get a quick snapshot of the most salient energies likely to impact the economic and market activities which are most closely associated with each individual horoscope.

THE FEDERAL RESERVE

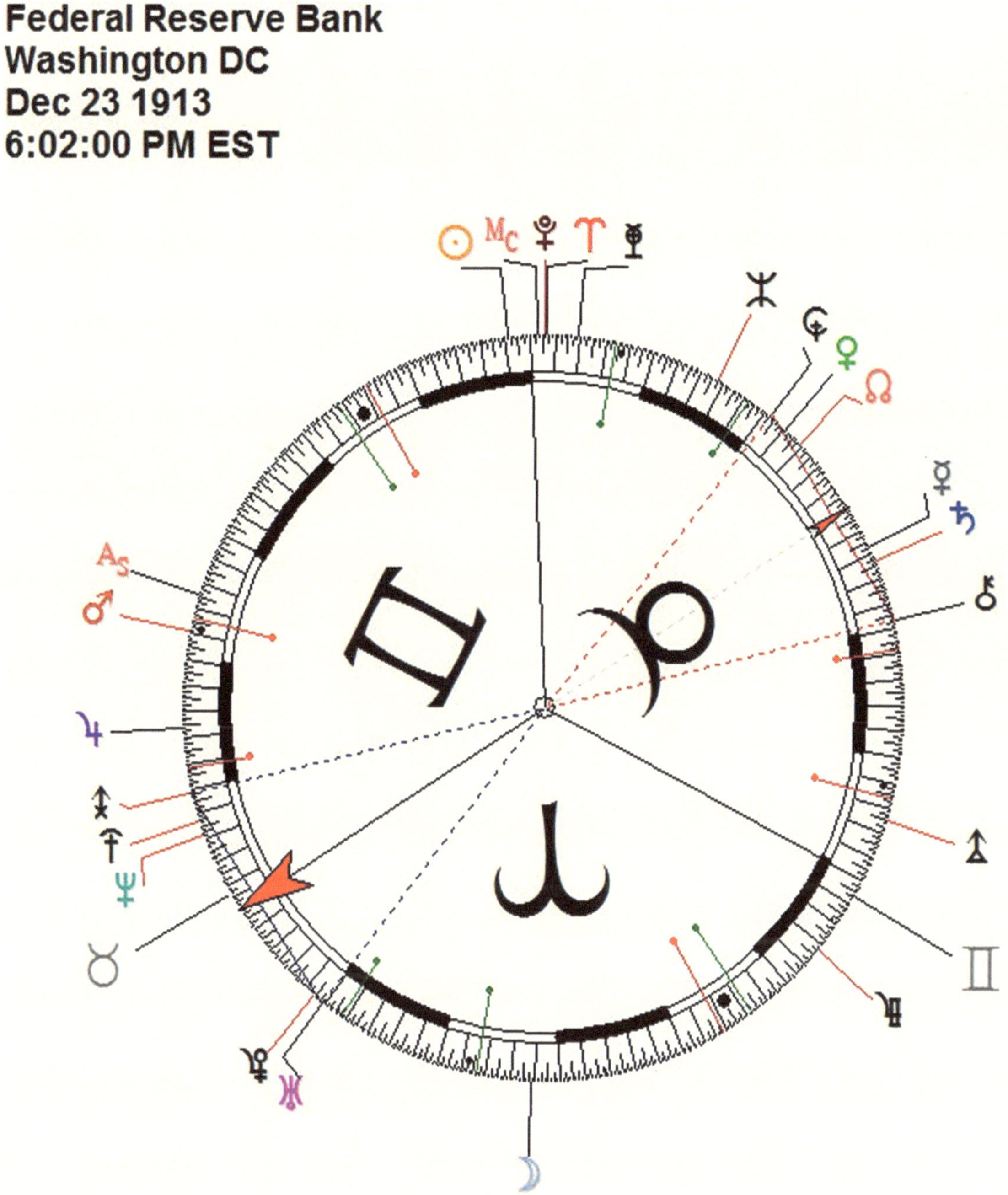

The Federal Reserve impacts the global economy and markets around the world more than any other financial entity. The October solar eclipse triggers the Fed's Uranus/Zeus midpoint, so we can expect surprisingly forccful actions from the central bank in the months after the eclipse. With the Chiron/Hades midpoint also in play, the Fed's actions may not be readily seen as favorable, but its handling of distasteful situations could ultimately prove beneficial, with a net positive economic outcome along the way.

NEW YORK STOCK EXCHANGE

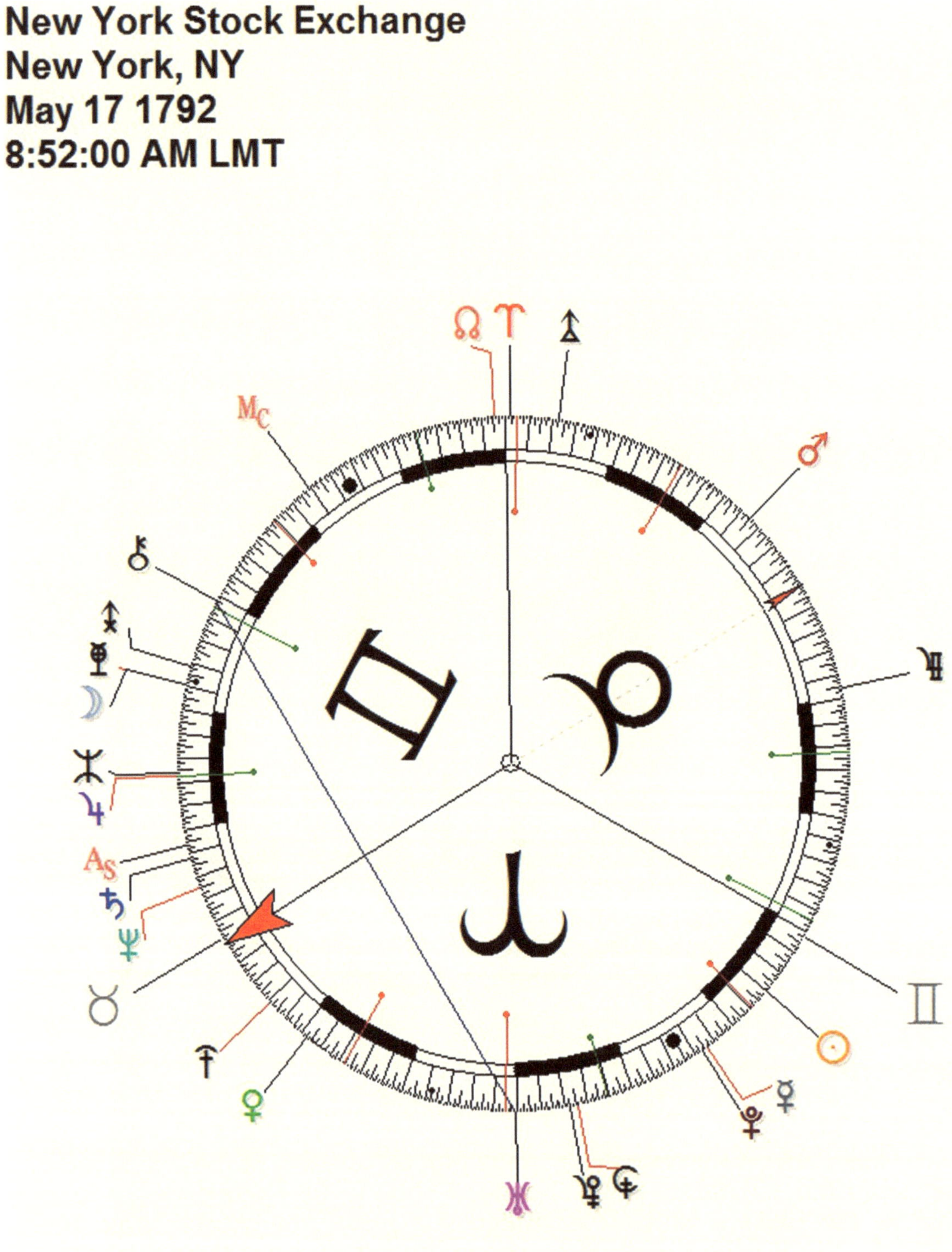

The activation of the NYSE Chiron/Uranus midpoint by the solar eclipse suggests unexpected problems in the trading environment for US stocks. The triggering of Saturn/Kronos hints of restrictive interventions by the Powers That Be, perhaps in response to a sudden market sell-off.

NASDAQ

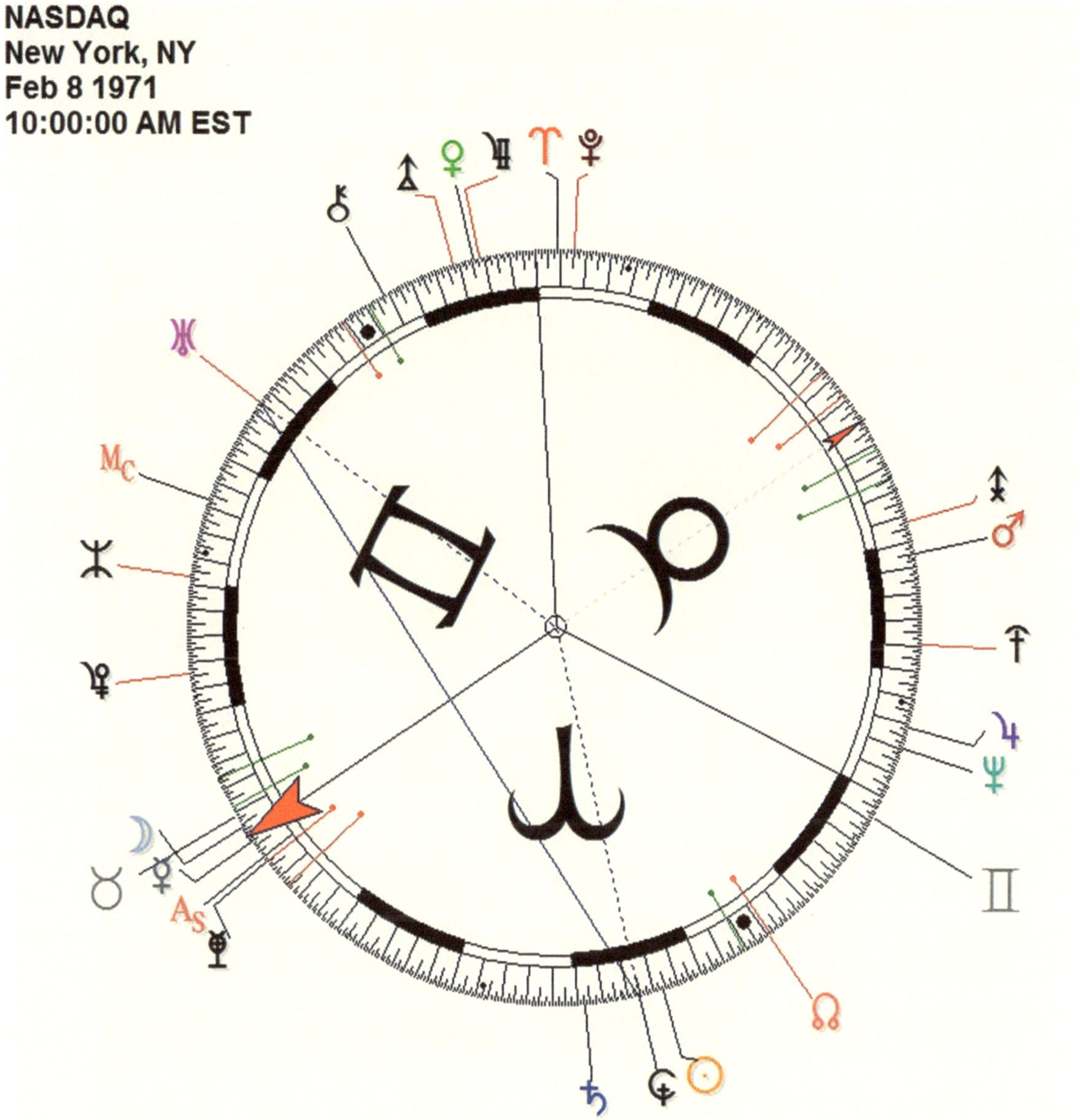

The outlook for the NASDAQ is a bit more ominous than that for the NYSE, mainly thanks to the solar eclipse activation of the Uranus/Hades midpoint. This can result in sudden extremely negative turns for the NASDAQ, especially since the eclipse activation of the Moon/Mercury midpoint is likely to keep reactive emotions running high. This could be an ideal set-up for short-term traders looking for a market advantage.

AUSTRALIAN STOCK EXCHANGE

Australian Stock Exchang
Sydney, Australia
Apr 1 1987
10:00:00 AM AEST

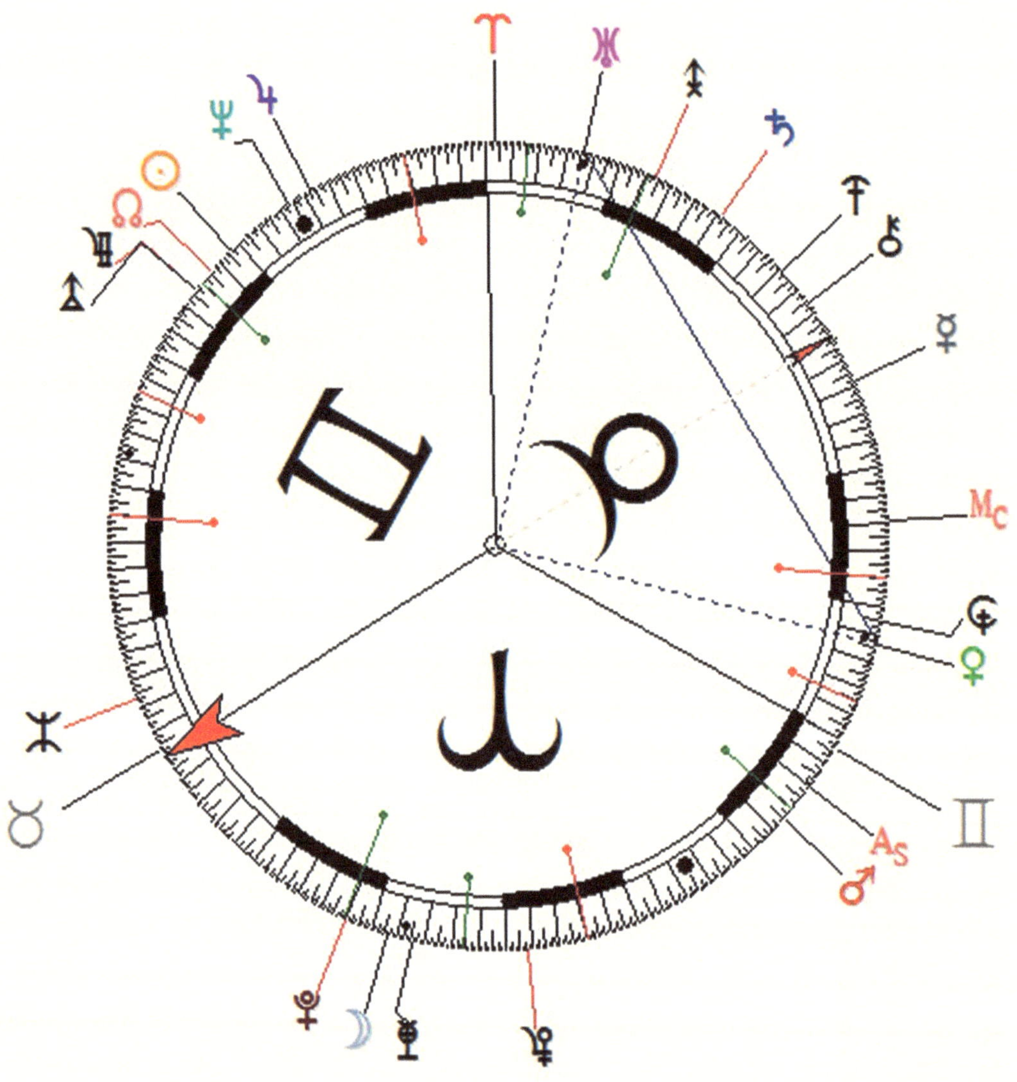

The impact on the Australian Stock Exchange resembles that on the NASDAQ, with Uranus/Hades triggered by the October eclipse. We don't see additional confirmations of a negative market, however, so traders need to be cautious about congestion as well as sudden pull-backs.

THE BOMBAY STOCK EXCHANGE

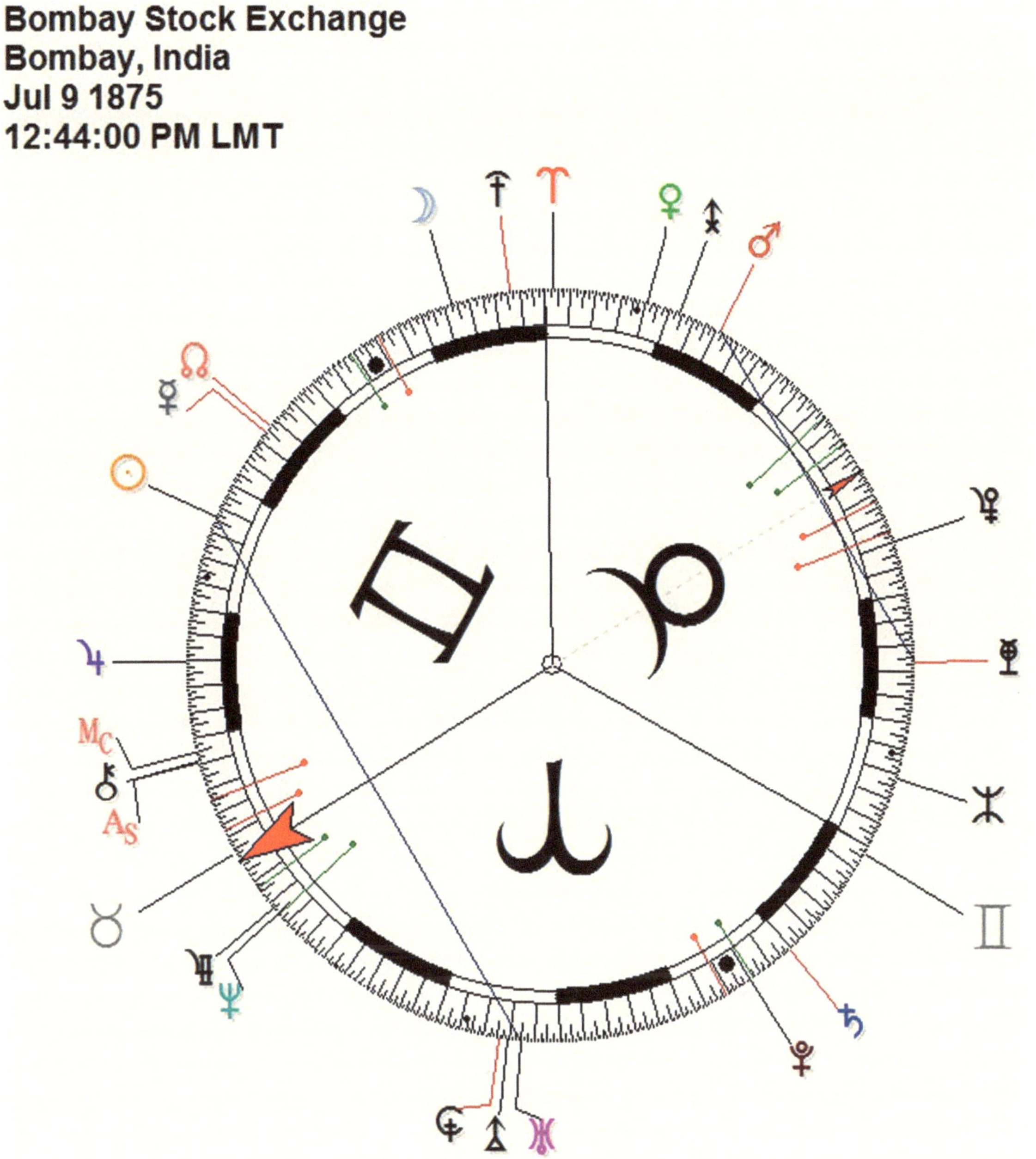

In spite of a restrictive Mars/Admetos activation which could slam the trading action dramatically, there are some positive indications in the months ahead for the stock market in India. The eclipse triggering of the Sun/Uranus midpoint structure could prove to be particularly beneficial to active traders in Indian equities during the months following the solar eclipse on October 23.

TREASURY BONDS

US Treasury Bonds
Chicago IL
Aug 22 1977
10:01:01 AM CDT

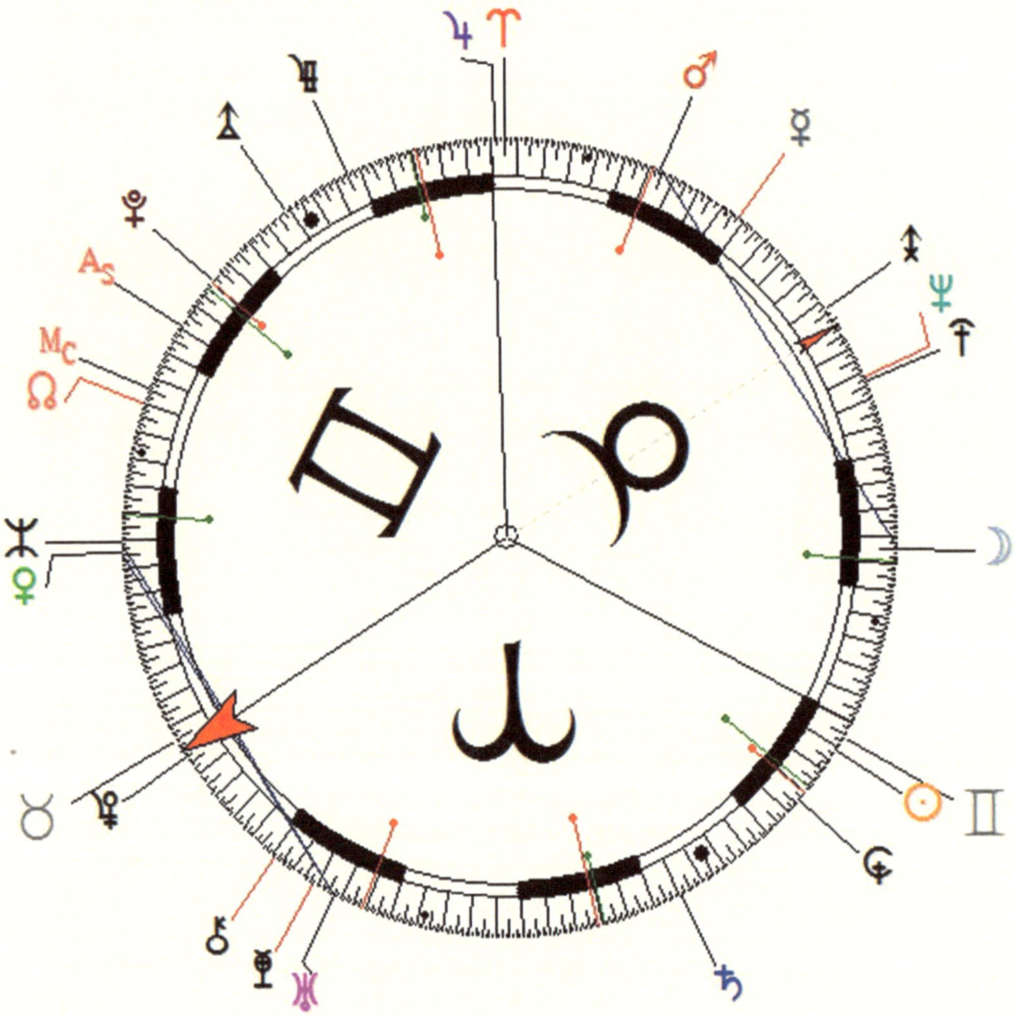

With the overall potential for stock market advances and improving economic conditions in the months ahead, it's possible that T-Bonds may start to look very attractive. That notion seems to be confirmed by the solar eclipse activation of the Moon/Mars mdpoint, stirring public attention, and the Venus/Uranus midpoint, a classic signature of surprisingly positive circumstances bringing unexpected opportunities.

THE U.S. DOLLAR

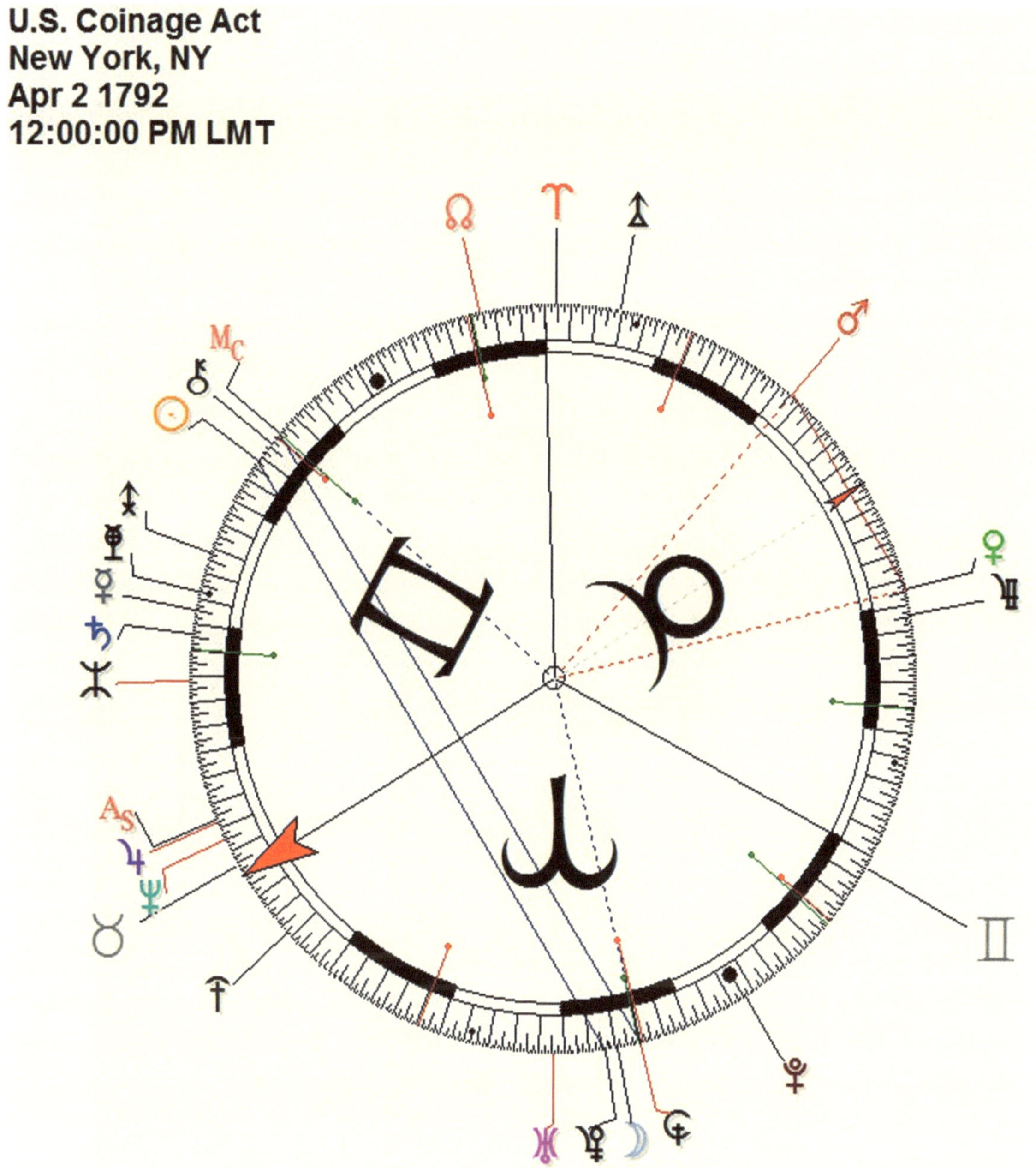

We are likely to see currency trading come under increasingly intense scrutiny during the months ahead, and with the solar eclipse activation of the Hades/Midheaven midpoint in the chart for the U.S. Dollar, that particular currency is likely to be a focal point. That doesn't necessarily mean a negative outcome for the greenback however – with the eclipse also triggering the Venus/Mars and Sun/Cupido midpoints, the immediate future is likely to be extremely positive for the dollar overall.

THE JAPANESE YEN

Japanese Yen
Tokyo, Tokyo
May 10 1871
12:00:00 PM LMT

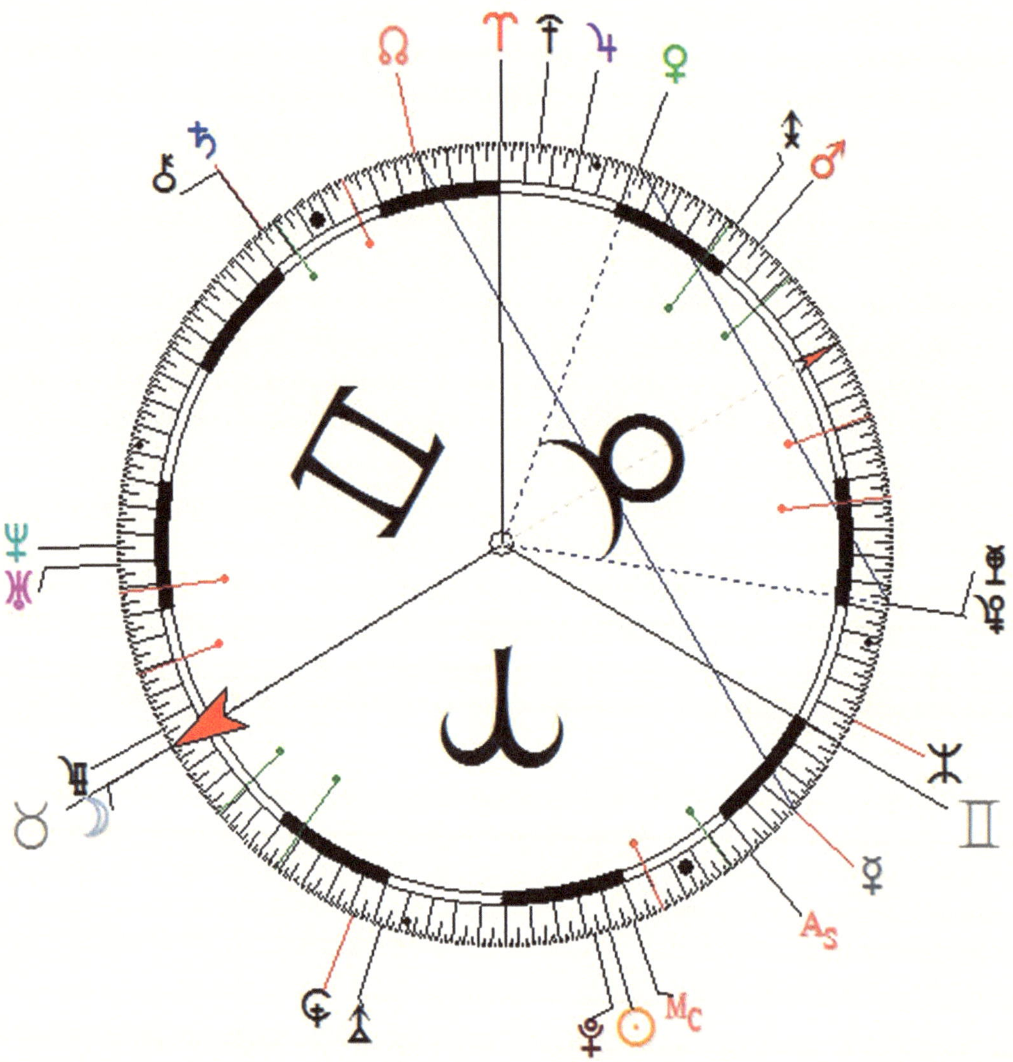

The October solar eclipse forms a precise square to the Moon in the chart for the Japanese yen, so public response to this currency will be especially important to watch. The outlook is mixed – the triggering of the Venus/Cupido and Mercury/Node midpoints suggest positive times ahead for this currency, but the activation of the Venus/Admetos midpoint could be enough to put the brakes on anything that looks like a sustained rally.

BITCOIN

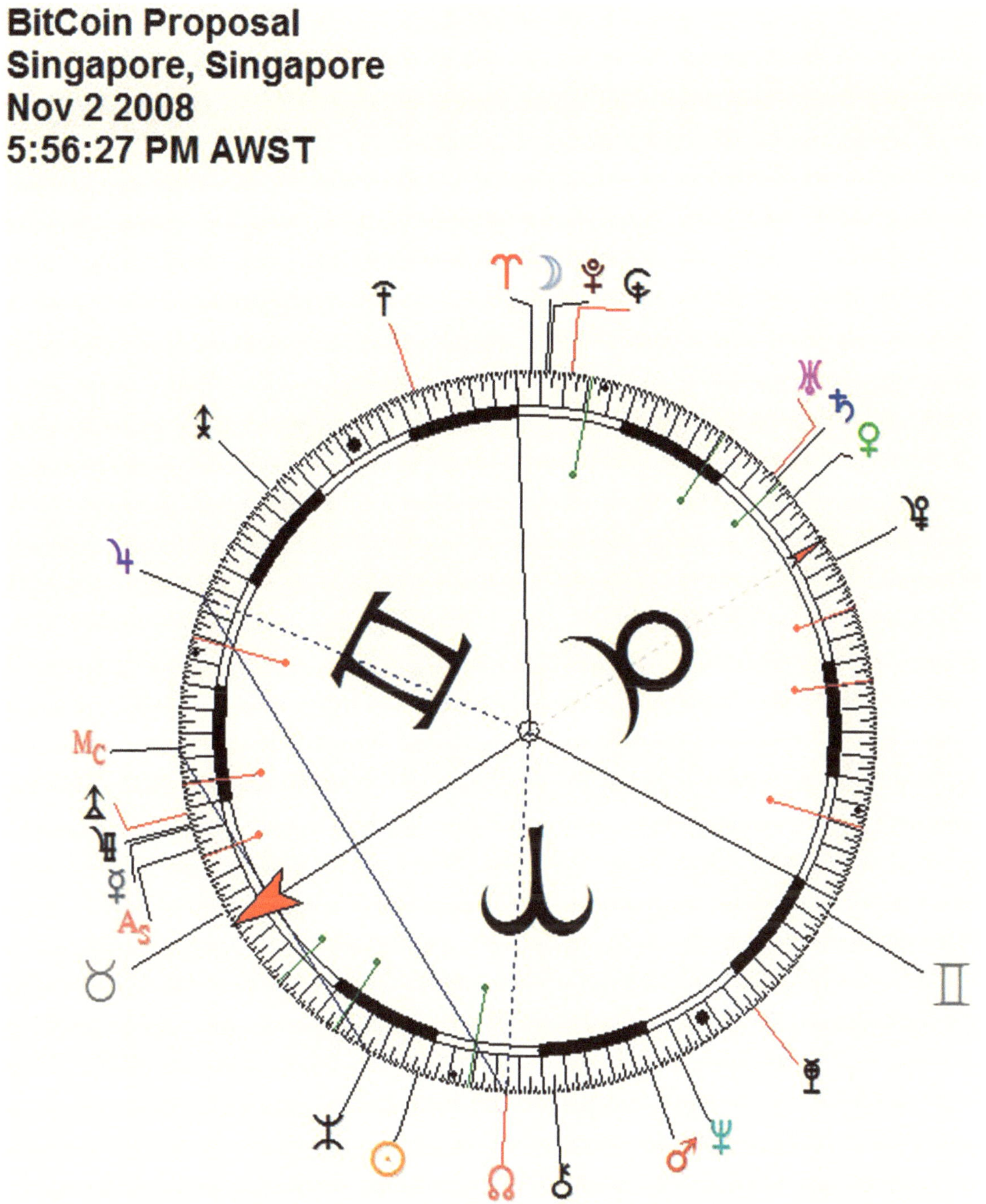

There continue to be solid astrological reasons for paying attention to the bitcoin crypto-currency, and with Apple and Google vying for dominance in digital currency, the eclipse activations of the Bitcoin Jupiter/Node and Midheaven/Poseidon midpoints are cause for optimism.

NYMEX LIGHT CRUDE OIL

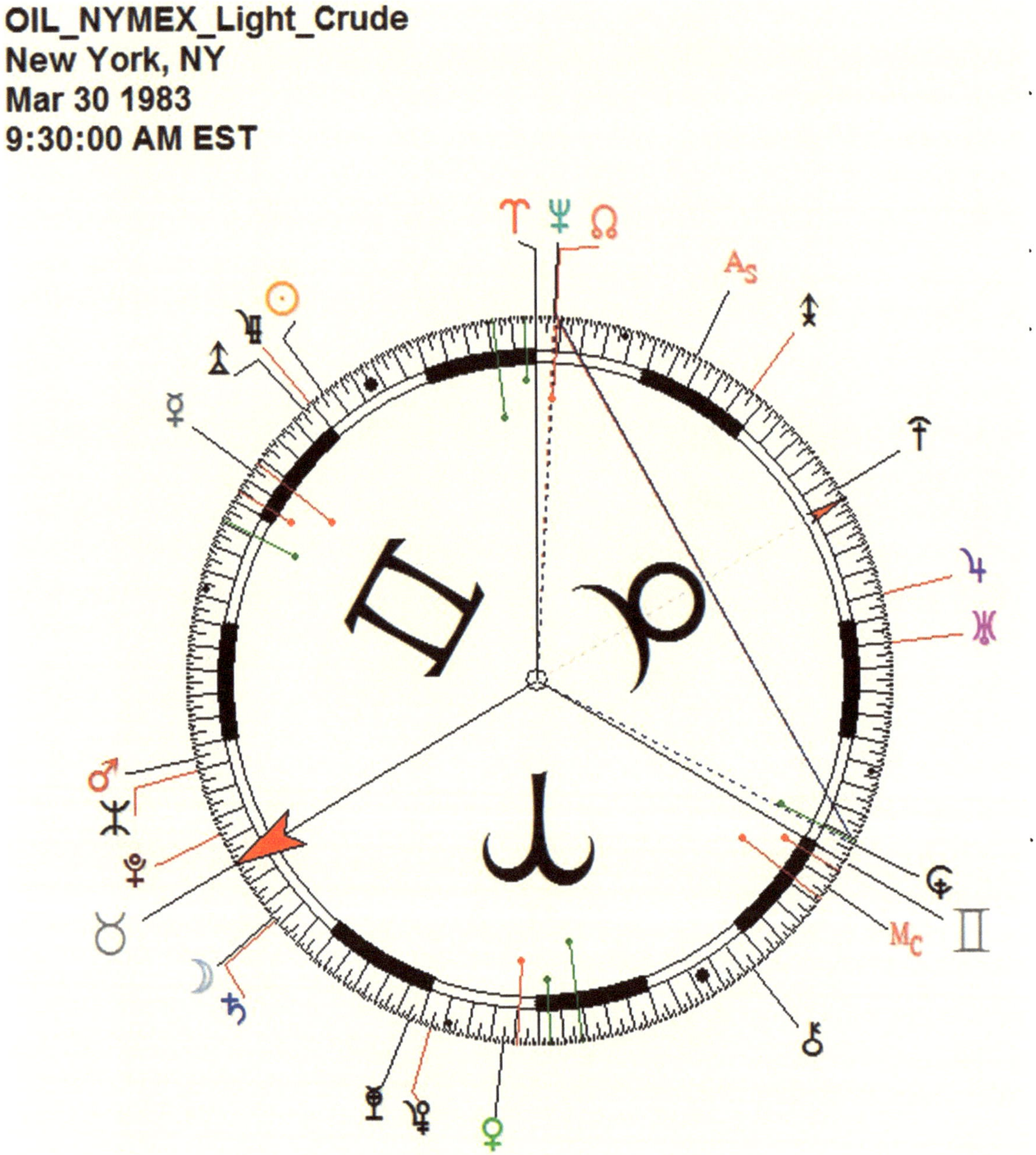

With the solar eclipse sesquiquadrate Kronos in the chart for NYMEX Light Crude, traders in this market will need to stay alert for regulatory actions which could skew prices. The Moon/Pluto activation suggests big moves in a fast market, but with Saturn/Pluto in the picture the tend for prices may tend to be lower instead of higher.

COMEX GOLD

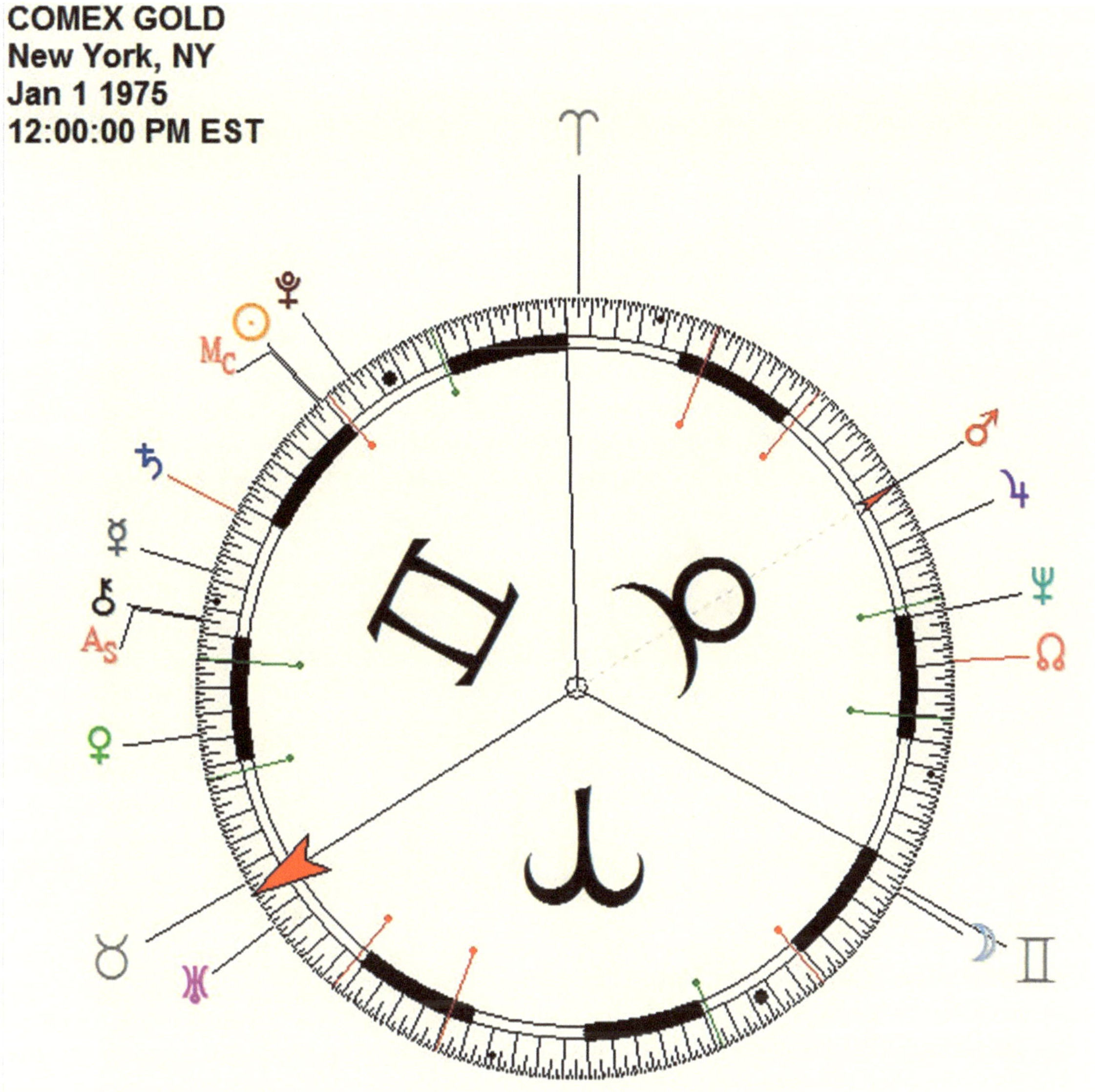

The impact of the October solar eclipse on the horoscope for COMEX Gold is very straightforward – the eclipse point forms a tight semi-square to Mars in that chart. Above all, this suggests that we could see some sustained market efforts to revive the yellow metal and return it to its former glory. With this kind of activation in play, it will be particularly important for Gold traders to watch the eclipse trigger dates that come up in the months following the eclipse, since they can provide a springboard for dramatic price moves. There's no guarantee, however, that Gold will be trading at its former highs during the next six or seven months. We may have to wait until after the next solar eclipse to see this tarnished metal shine again.

COMEX SILVER

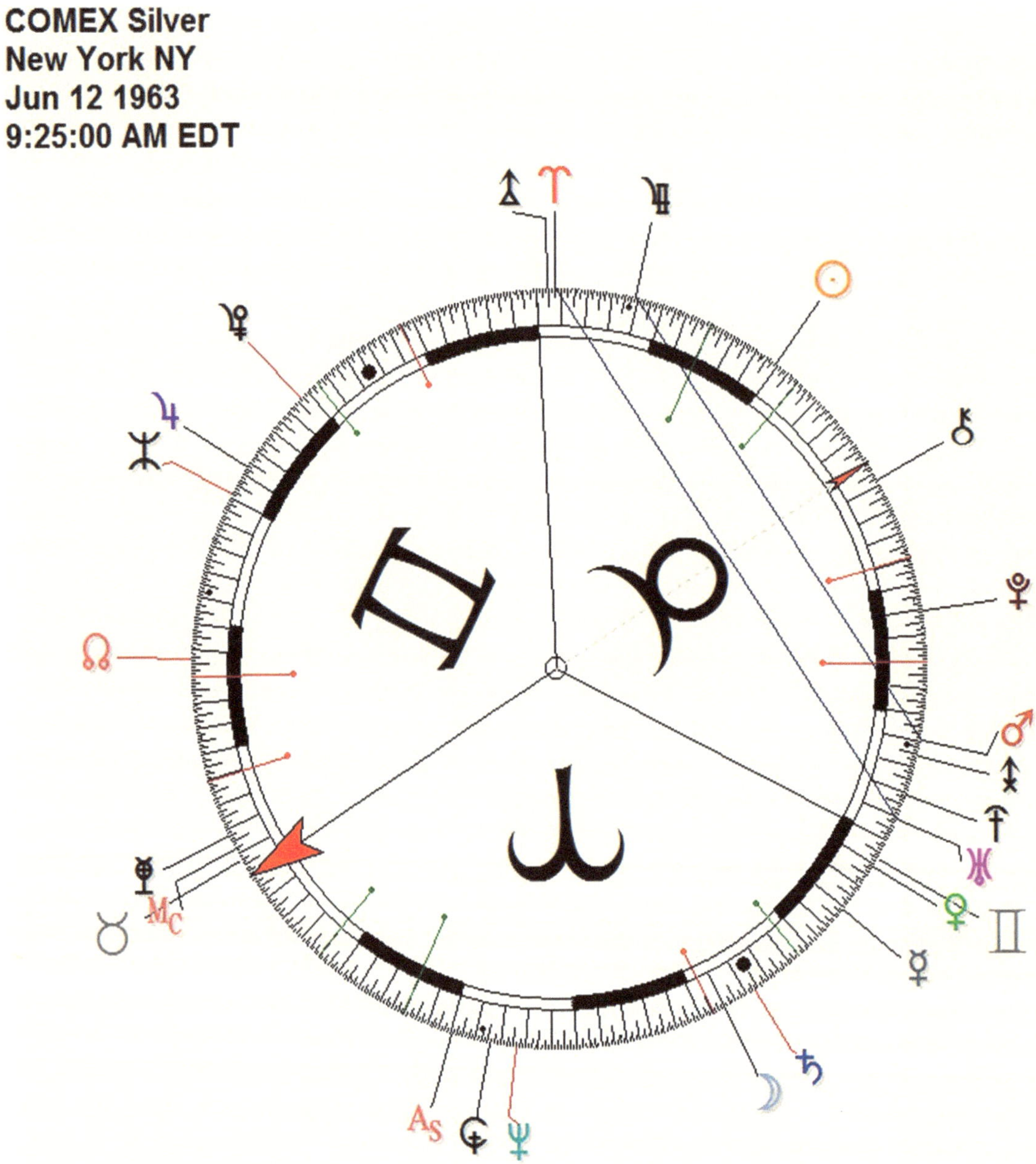

Traders who are eager to get back into bullish positions in the precious metals may find better prospects with Silver than with Gold during the coming months. The October solar eclipse triggers the Midheaven in COMEX Silver chart, thrusting this metal into the spotlight. The activation of the Zeus/Apollon midpoint sets an extremely positive tone for speculation in this metal, and with the Uranus/Aries Point midpoint in play as well, we could see Silver become the center of attention on a global scale.

Lunar Returns to the Solar Eclipse

The impact of the October 23 solar eclipse is not limited solely to the date when it takes place. From an astrological perspective, the eclipse event creates a powerful resonant field that continues to provide noteworthy opportunities for the eclipse energy to be activated well into the future—at least until the time of the next solar eclipse, which in this case comes on March 20, 2015.

This resonant field operates through the zodiacal points at which the eclipse occurs and also through the antiscion (also known as the solstice point) of the eclipse. With the October solar eclipse coming at 00° 24' Scorpio the eclipse antiscion falls at 29° 36' Aquarius.

One of the ways that we can best see the resonant field at work during the months following the eclipse is by tracking the series of Lunar Returns to the October solar eclipse. Each Lunar Return is set for the exact time that the Moon returns to the position it held at the time of the solar eclipse.

In general, Lunar Returns to solar eclipses often mark significant points in the markets, so they are worth watching as potential triggers for trend reversals and shifts in market momentum. While solar eclipse Lunar Returns don't impact all markets in an identical manner, they are nevertheless an extremely valuable key to unlocking the hidden dynamics that can move the markets in powerful ways.

Each Lunar Return relates to the solar eclipse as a resonating factor, which is what helps to provoke the kinds of trend reversals that we see so often in association with these events, but it can also be considered by itself as a separate and significant moment in time.

Considering each solar eclipse Lunar Return as a separate event has the advantage of providing us with an emotional index of the month ahead, so we can get some insight into what is most likely to impact market trends during the four-week period following each lunar return.

As we do so, we are getting an overview of general market tendencies rather than a specific forecast of particular trends or turning points. Even so, this can provide valuable background information as we fine tune our market forecasts each month and as we look for specific trading opportunities during the course of each trading week throughout the six-month period following the solar eclipse.

November 20, 2014

The initial lunar return to the October solar eclipse comes on November 20, 2013. With mutable signs on the angles of this horoscope, we can expect a fluid market environment, but that environment is more likely to promote price consolidation then aggressive bullishness or a sustained rally.

With the Moon in the second house of this chart, financial matters and concerns about essential value are likely to be sources of major stress, both in and out of the markets. While the conjunction of Zeus and the True Lunar Node suggests active participation in trading and negotiations, the trine between Neptune and Hades provides a clear warning that speculation can lead to severe disappointment at this time.

All the planetary action in this chart is disposited by a mutual reception between Mars and Saturn, indicating that efforts to push forward are met with obstacles, while attempts to create plans and structures come apart under pressure from the need to take immediate action.

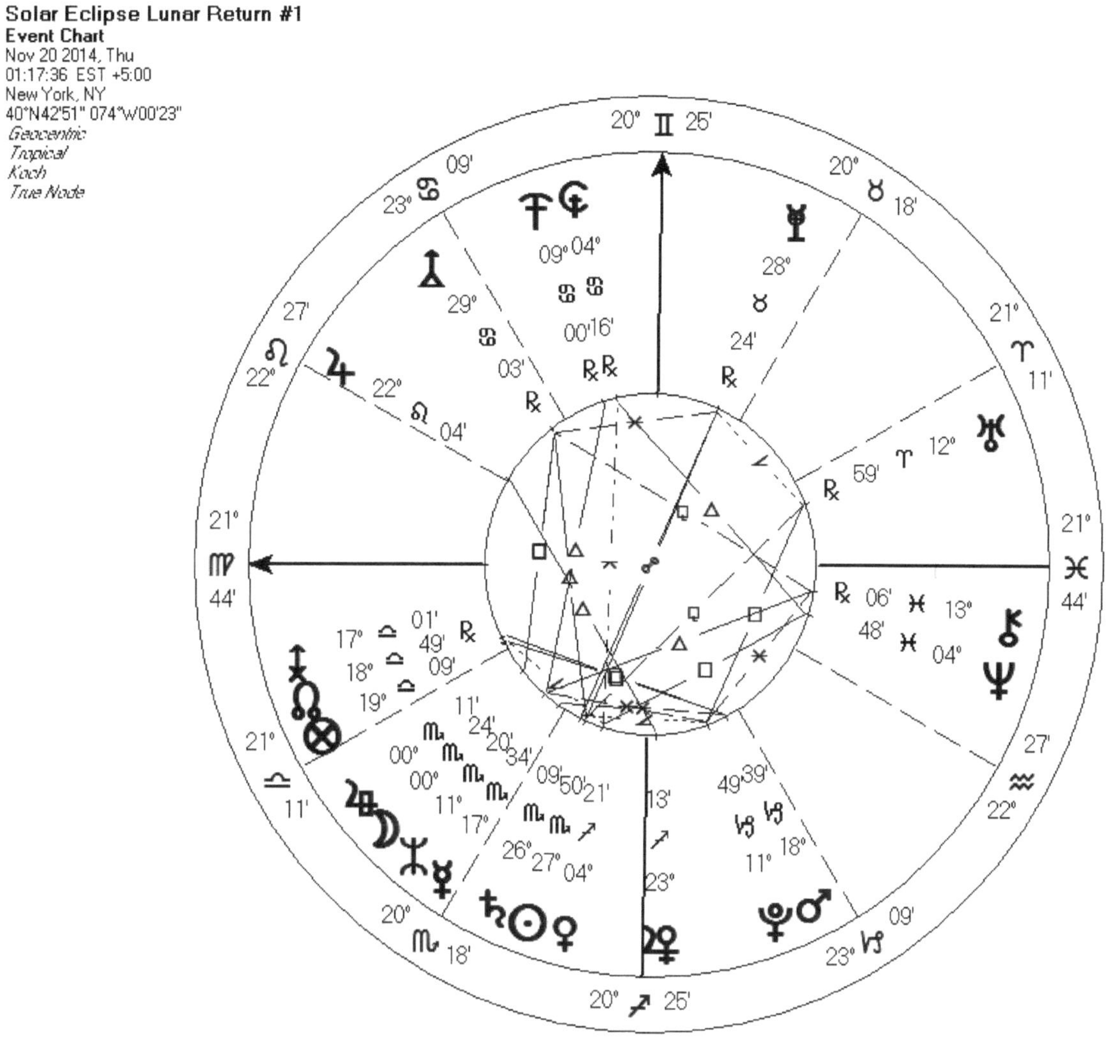

Perhaps the best strategy for traders during the end of November and the first couple of weeks of December will be to heed the warning provided by Saturn as the ruler of the fifth house of risk-taking in this horoscope – it tells us to exercise considerable caution with any trades we enter.

December 17, 2014

The lunar return to the solar eclipse on December 17, 2014 comes a particularly potent time. It takes place just two days after the final waxing Uranus/Pluto square of 2014, with those planets occupying two of the key money houses in this horoscope. With Mercury ruling the fifth house in the chart, there's a lot of interest in taking market positions during the closing days of 2014 and the opening weeks of 2015, but because Mercury is in the 11th house in this horoscope, the emphasis for most traders is likely to be more on the potential for the profits that can be had by participating in the markets rather than on the risks that come along with market involvement.

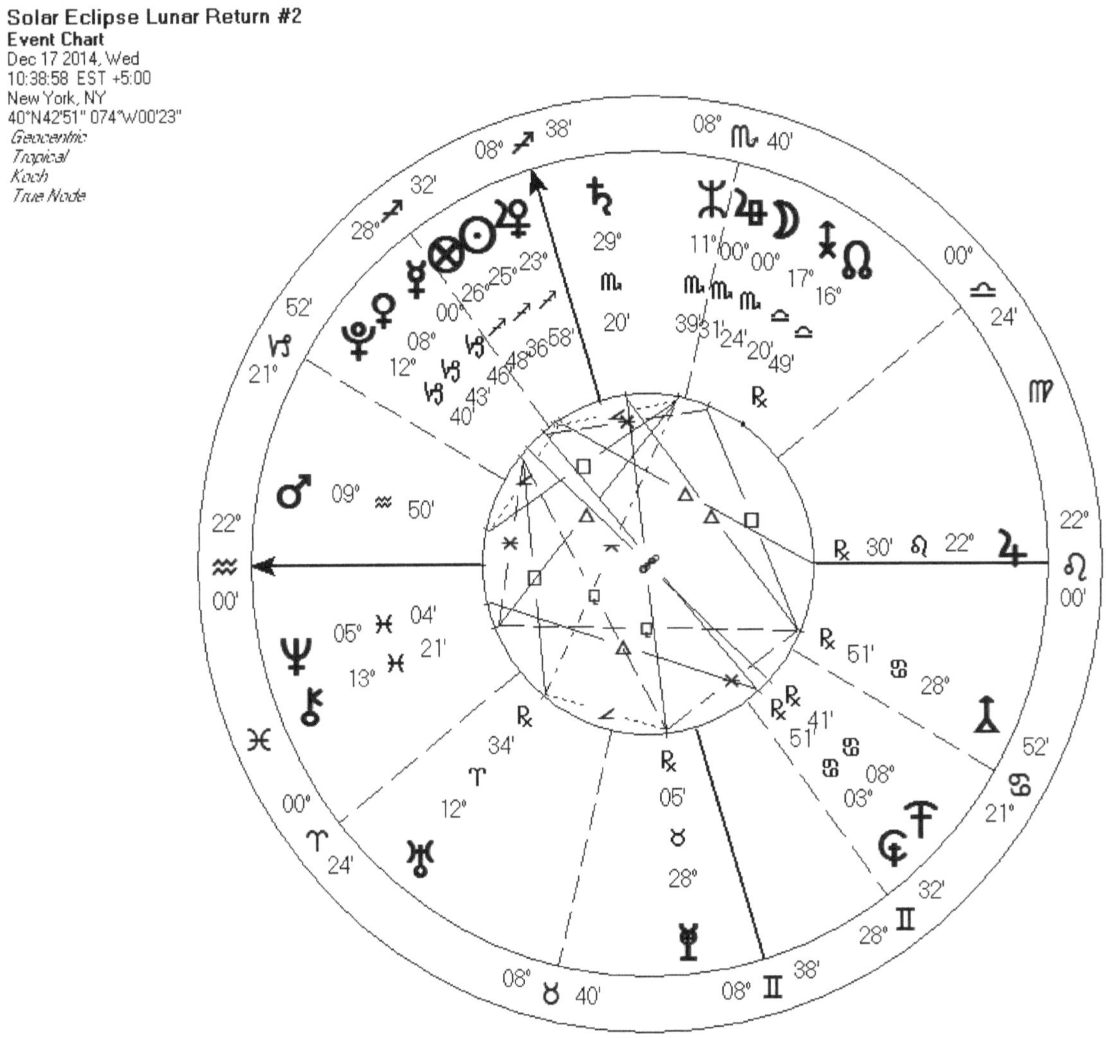

That's a particularly dangerous attitude for the trader to take, and this lunar return gives us a great reminder that the current situation is no exception – with the transneptunians Hades and Kronos in the fifth house of the chart, traders are quite likely to confront big disappointments and severe limitations if they try to move too far too fast at this time.

With Jupiter on the cusp of the seventh house in the horoscope, it will be easy to think about trading partners as cooperative parties rather than as adversaries in the markets. But with Virgo intercepted in the seventh house of the chart, there's a strong tendency to misjudge the corresponding parties in any trading dynamic, so traders at any level of experience would do well to bring an extra level of caution to their market engagements at this time.

With the Moon in the eighth house of the horoscope, there's a strong emphasis here on indebtedness, so it will be especially important to pay attention to the use of margin at this time. While using margin in a brokerage account can add leverage for more powerful trading, it can also become a trap that sucks up capital resources which may be better directed in other ways.

This horoscope is also unusual because the planetary action in the chart is disposited by two separate mutual receptions. Neptune yields its energy to Jupiter, which is in a mutual reception with the Sun. This combination creates a potential for an optimistic attitude toward the benefits that can come with trading at this time. But the chart's second mutual reception, between Mars and Saturn, resonates strongly with the previous lunar return and gives us a much more realistic reminder of the true limits that we are likely to encounter in the markets as we bring the year to a close.

January 13, 2015

The third lunar return to the solar eclipse, and the first such lunar return of 2015, comes on January 13, with fixed signs of the zodiac on the angles of the horoscope. This fixed dynamic within the context of planetary energies creates the kind of potential stalemate that the word itself implies – fixed energy doesn't go anywhere at all, because its natural tendency is to avoid change.

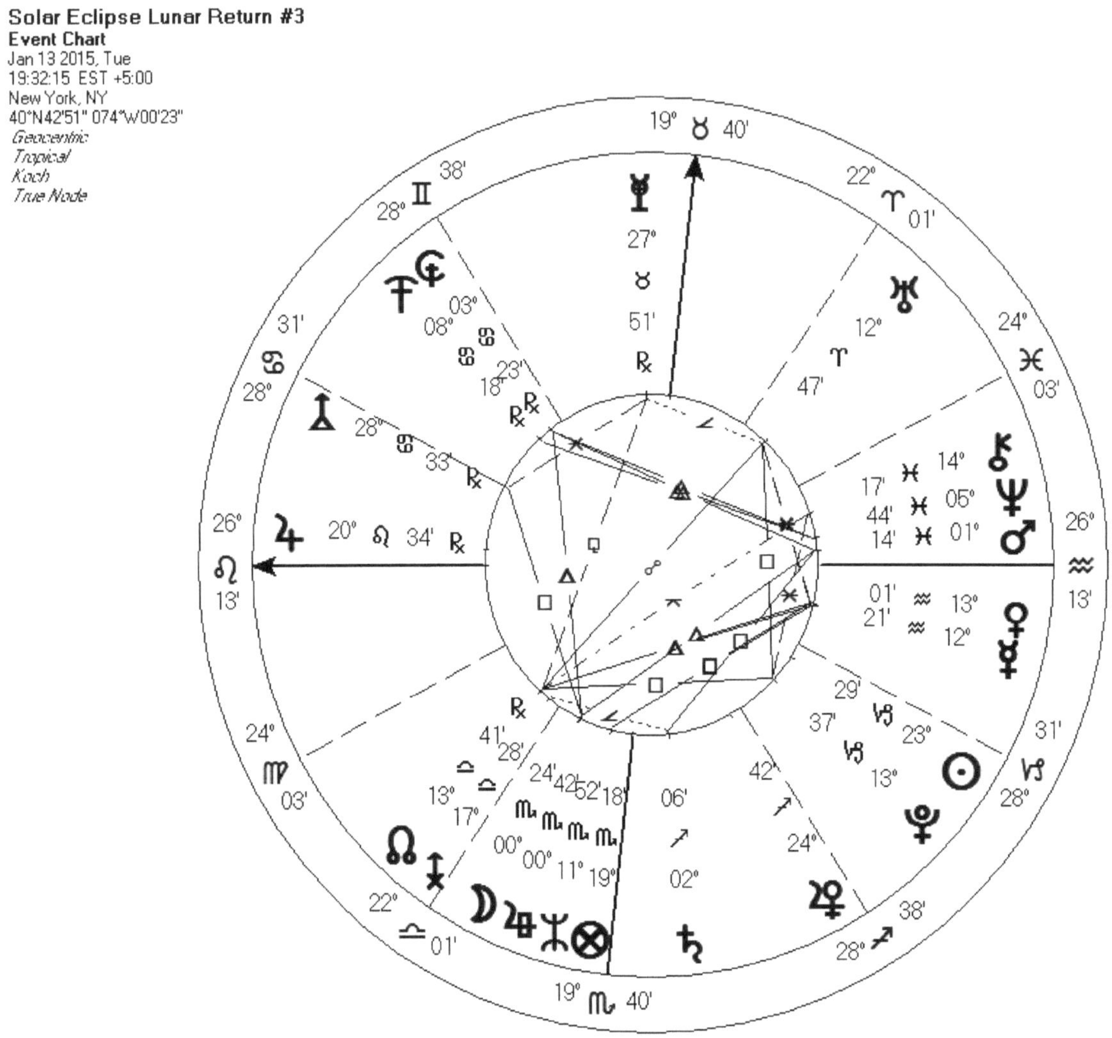

That potential for stagnation is reflected elsewhere in the chart, with the Moon posited in the third house suggesting that it will be a lot easier to think about trading than to take decisive action in the markets.

The Grand Trine in the chart, between the conjunction of the Moon and Apollon in Scorpio, Hades in Cancer, and Mars in Pisces, gives us an emphasis on the emotional energy associated with the zodiac's water signs. This emotional undercurrent provides a potential tinderbox for the energies expressed through the fifth house of the horoscope. With Jupiter ruling that zone of the chart, and with both the Sun and Pluto posited in that house, there will be a strong tendency on the part of some individuals to over-trade in late January and early February, acting powerfully and impulsively as an emphatic antidote to extended periods of compulsive inaction.

Note that Jupiter, the ruler of the fifth, is in the 12th house in this chart, suggesting that a fear of being left out of the market action can itself become a motivator for precipitous risk-taking. Nevertheless, the predominance of static energy in this chart suggests that the overall trading environment is considerably more likely to promote market congestion than to exhibit a strongly-defined trading trend during the the closing weeks of January and the opening days of February in 2015.

February 10, 2015

The lunar return of February 10, 2015, with the Moon in the 11th house of the horoscope, features a strong emphasis on the potential rewards that can come with risk-taking in the markets. The tendency that's highlighted here will provoke many traders to pay a lot of attention to the situations that have generated inadequate returns on investments, with a nagging sense of failure in reaping appropriate profits from treating positions.

Mars is the ruler of the fifth house in this chart, but there is no final dispositor to the horoscope, so the energy expressed by the planets flows in circles rather than moving in a vectored direction toward decisive action. With Mars posited in the third house of the chart in the intercepted sign of Pisces, traders are likely to experience a tendency to think about trading, talk about trading, and then, if they do any actual trading at all, to act on the basis of hunches and intuition rather than following a well-structured trading plan.

With Mercury in retrograde motion at the time of this lunar return, it will be a good opportunity to review brokerage accounts, to make sure that financial records are in order, and to restructure specific trading plans. It will also be an excellent time for opening up new educational horizons and for expanding knowledge of the markets.

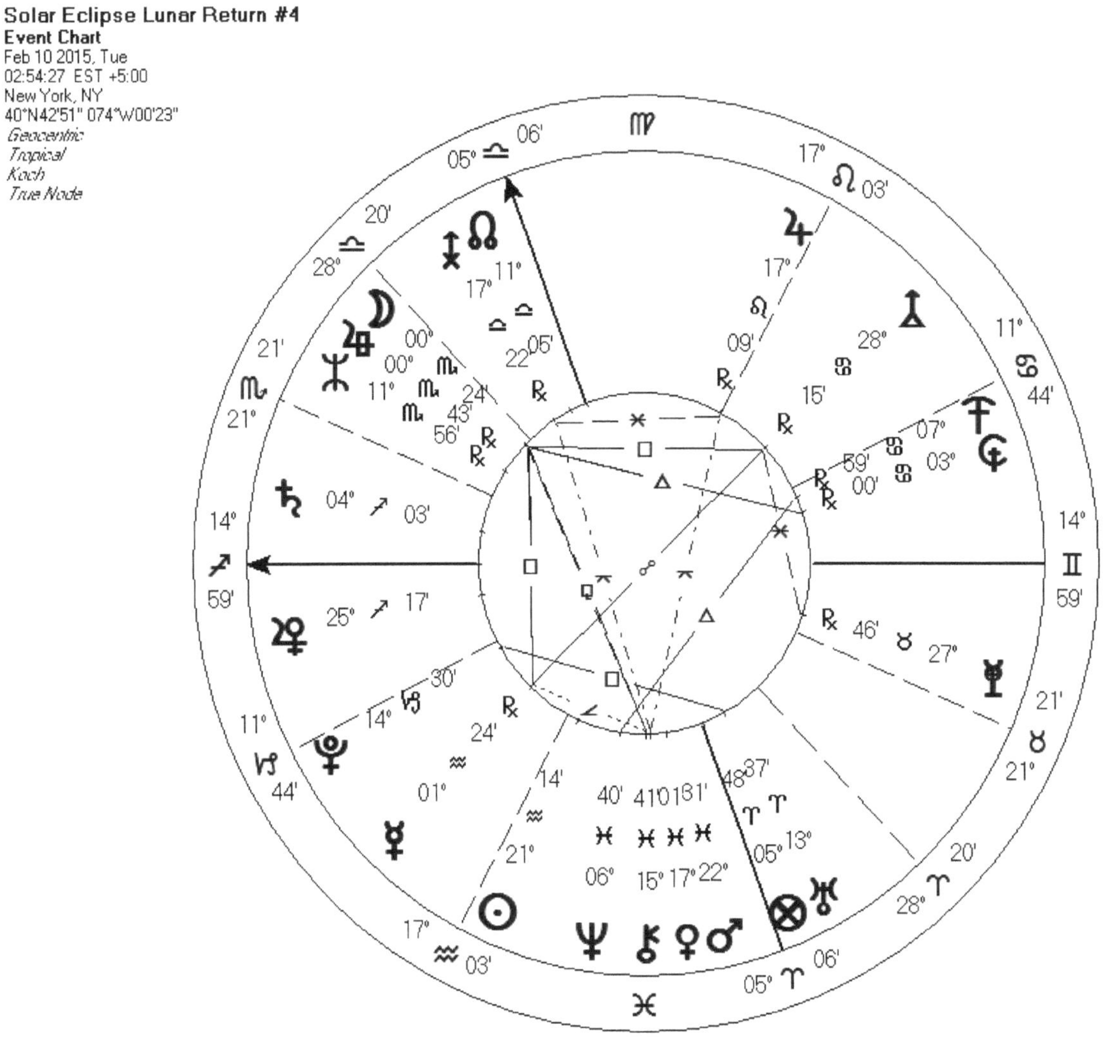

Venus in Pisces, Zeus in Libra, and Jupiter in Leo combine their forces in this chart to create a well-defined yod, or “finger of fate” pattern, suggesting that energetic and enthusiastic engagement with the markets at this time can create rich intellectual rewards, and perhaps some handsome financial rewards as well.

March 9, 2015

On March 9, 2015, the fifth lunar return to the solar eclipse takes place with the fixed signs of the zodiac on the angles of the horoscope chart for the lunar return. This chart tells us that the biggest challenge of the final three weeks of March and the first few days of April will be to stay focused on the routine, day-to-day tasks that need to be performed on a regular basis in order to adhere to a specific trading plan effectively. There will be plenty of opportunities for distraction at this time, as is demonstrated by the tremendous amount of energy expressed in this horoscope

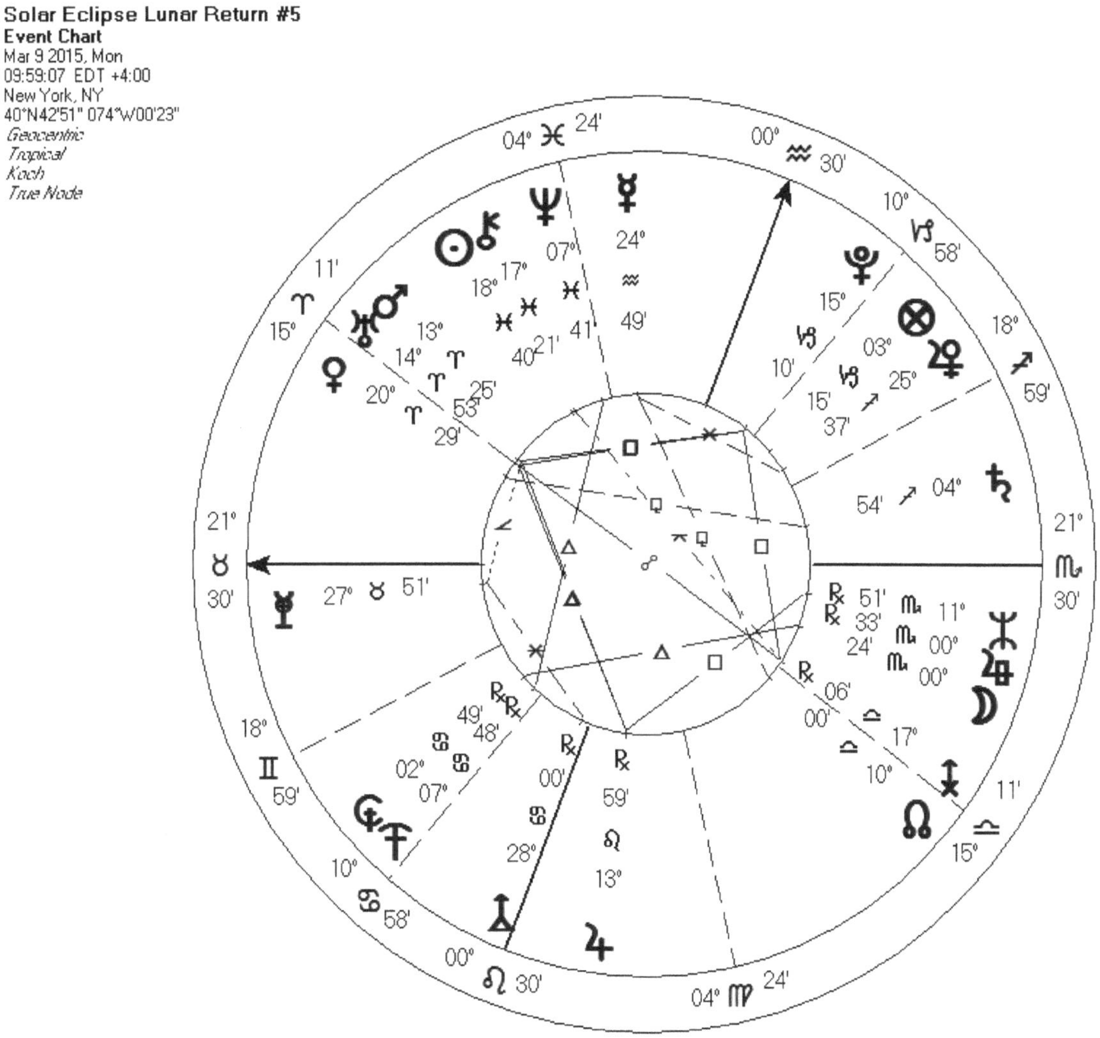

A glance at the 11th house of the horoscope reveals a conjunction of Mars and Uranus. This planetary combination is the epitome of explosive energy, so it will be quite easy for traders to be pulled away from mundane or routine considerations and become obsessed with heroic efforts solely designed to create more income.

That volatile Mars/Uranus configuration would probably be enough to keep most market participants hopping for the entire month, but this horoscope doesn't stop there with its energetic expressions. Mercury is the ruler of the fifth house of speculation here, and it is located in the 10th house of the chart in a sesquiquadrate to the True Lunar Node. This alignment suggests a strong compulsion toward connecting with other people at this time, an activity which can certainly bring about productive consequences, but which can also become a potential diversion from disciplined trading.

Note that the planetary energies in this chart get funneled into two directions. Mercury, Saturn, Neptune, and Pluto all send their force into a mutual reception of the Sun and Jupiter, resolving some of the horoscope's most powerful impulses into feel-good acts of self-congratulation. The remainder of the planets in the chart are all disposited by Mars, which, as we have already pointed out, is in a tight conjunction with Uranus, amplifying this planet's highly-directed energy enormously. And to top things off, this lunar return occurs just a few days before the seventh and final precise alignment of the waxing Uranus/Pluto square series, which has dominated market activities, interpersonal relationships, and geopolitical alignments during the past several years, and which will continue to have a residual effect for some time to come.

In short, this is a chart that expresses an enormous amount of energy which is likely to be exhibited quite dramatically in the market environment. While there are some indications here of inhibited efforts at expansion, they are so completely overwhelmed astrologically by the high-energy components of the chart that we strongly anticipate a time of exuberant bullishness in the markets for late March and early April.

April 5, 2015

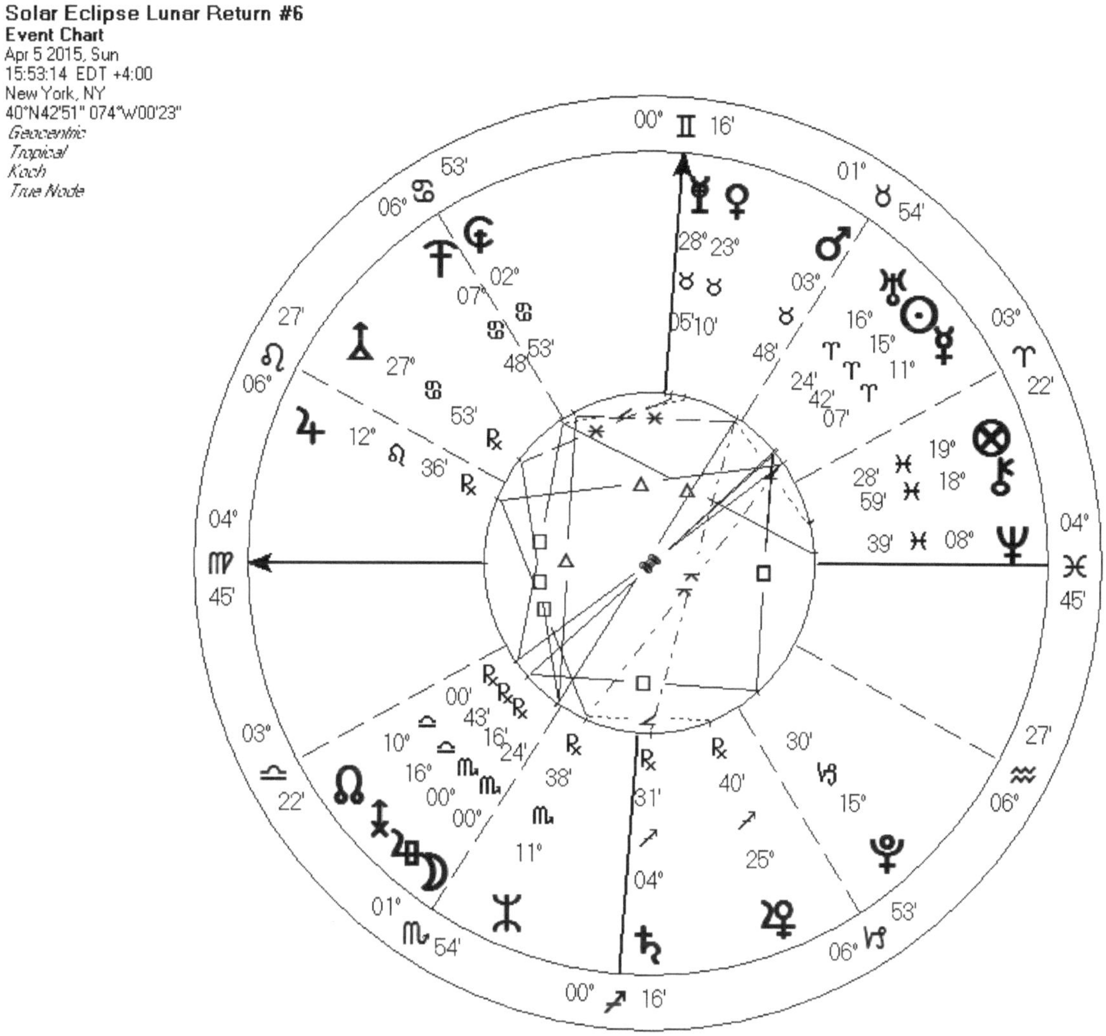

On April 5, 2015, the lunar return to the solar eclipse creates a horoscope with mutable zodiac signs on the angles of the chart. This indicates a time for shifting trends in the markets, and if the previous lunar return cycle has indeed resulted in the kind of powerful market rally we anticipate, we can expect the lunar return dynamics in April to slow the bull down a bit. By this time, the next solar eclipse, which arrives on March 20, 2015, will also be making its influence felt, which may add an additional tempering action in the markets.

This is not to say, however, that trading on the long side of the market can't be profitable at this time. Although the Moon's position in the second house of the chart suggests the likelihood of financial worries, the final dispositor of this horoscope is Venus, one of the classical money planets and forceful indicator of financial well-being. It's worth noting here that Venus in this chart this disposits Mars, which in turn receives the energy of the Sun, the Moon, Mercury, and Uranus, so that the intense energetic expression of the red planet is directed toward worthwhile results. Harnessing these planetary dynamics in the markets can give astro-traders a significant advantage at this time.

We are moving away from the the whole Uranus/Pluto square series as this lunar return unfolds, but that planetary dynamic is still very much in evidence through a T-square pattern in this horoscope. Pluto in the fifth house of the chart is at the apex of the pattern, which is formed with Zeus in the second house and the Sun/Uranus conjunction in the eighth house of the chart. This powerful configuration can motivate some highly productive trading action, suggesting that this will be a profitable time to look for buying opportunities in the markets. Note, however, that Saturn is the ruler of the fifth house in this chart, so a cautious and well-structured trading plan and clearly conservative attitudes toward risk-taking will be essential for traders at this time.

May 2, 2015

The final lunar return for the solar eclipse that we will consider in this monograph takes place on May 2, 2015. Note that this is well after the next solar eclipse, which takes place on March 20, 2015. Even so, the effects of solar elcipses tend to overlap, with the impact of one eclipse waning as a new eclipse comes into the picture. We thus have reason to believe that the October solar eclipse will still be making its influence felt at this time, so we have included this lunar return horoscope for reference.

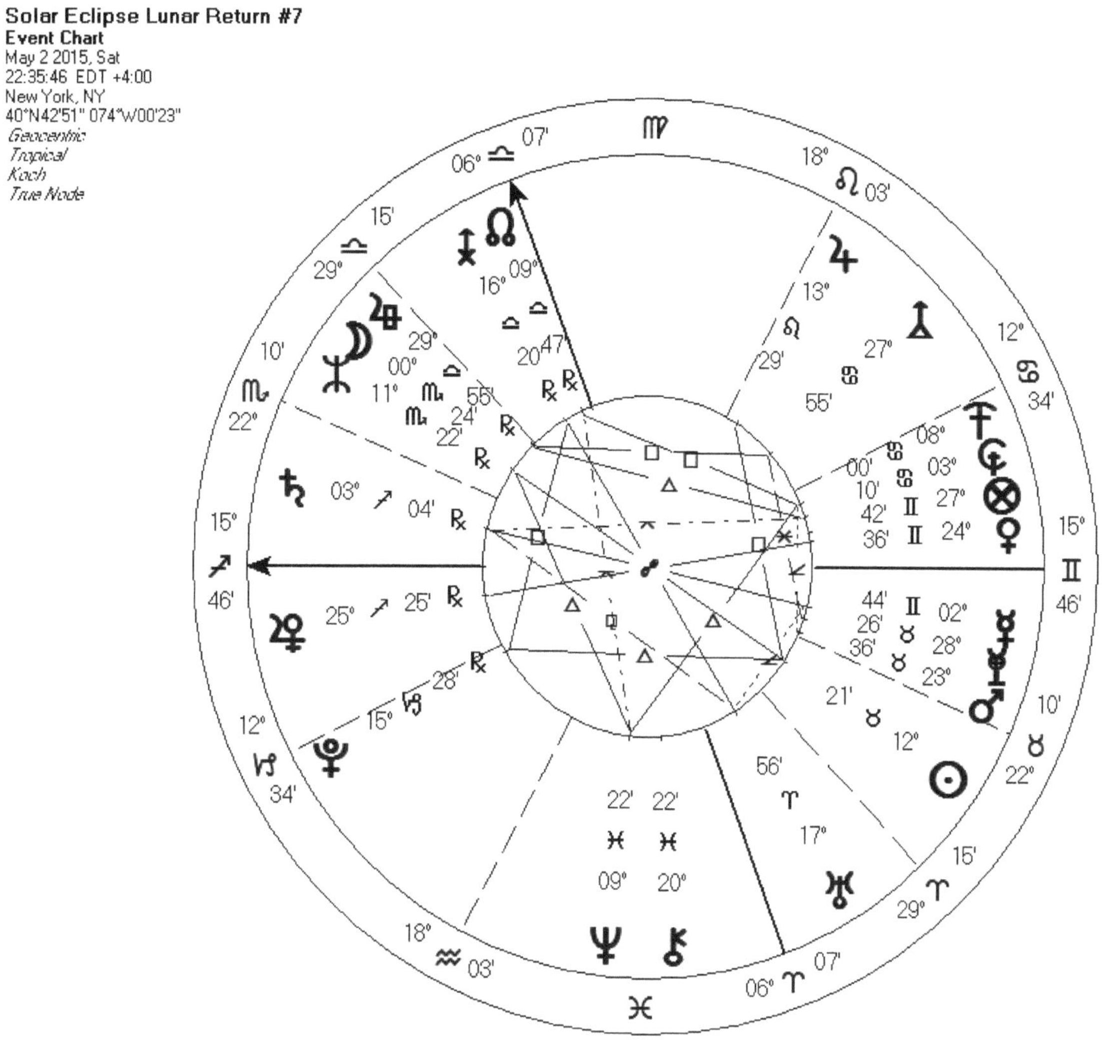

The Moon, which is almost full, is in the 11th house of this horoscope, suggesting potential tensions based on desires for enhanced returns from speculative activities. The Sun is in the fifth house, indicating a strong pull toward risk-taking and speculation in general, and with Mars as the ruler of the fifth house, that attraction is likely to find ample outward expression.

With Mars in the sixth house of this horoscope, it should be relatively easy for traders to maintain active engagement in the markets throughout the month of May. But while we can anticipate a rising market trend during that month, bringing some clear possibilities for significant profits, it's worth noting here that all the energies in this chart ultimately resolve themselves into a mutual reception between Mercury and Venus. The never-ending exchange of energy expressed through the mutual reception between these two planets suggests that it may be difficult for traders to feel a sense of satisfaction about the results of their trading during this month, regardless of how successfully their efforts are reflected on their balance sheets by the end of May.

There could be some challenges, then, for some traders in heeding the traditional advice to "sell in May and go away." If they choose to hold on to their positions past the end of the month, however, it will be the solar eclipse of March 20, 2015 that is likely to have the biggest influence on their success in the markets through the summer months.

This chart offers one additional consideration that is worth noting here. The fifth-house Sun in the chart, while offering a strong focus on risk-taking, trading, and speculative behavior in general, is square the midpoint of Neptune and Pluto in the horoscope.

This sounds another cautionary note that traders should pay attention to – it's a configuration that suggests powerful and potentially duplicitous forces at work behind the scenes, bringing additional risk exposure to those who fail to do their due diligence in examining trading opportunities.

It will be all too easy to overlook potential market booby-traps as this planetary configuration is in effect, so before committing any money in a new trading position in May, the wise trader will take the time to ask, "Exactly what am I missing here?"

The Eclipse Point, Antiscion, and Two-Eclipse Midpoint

In anticipating the potential effects of the October 2014 solar eclipse, we can work not only with upcoming transits to the eclipse point and its antiscion at 29° 36' Aquarius and with Lunar Returns for the eclipse horoscope, but also with transits to the positions of the planets, Chiron, and the Transneptunians in the solar eclipse horoscope.

We also want to be aware of 14° 56' Capricorn as a sensitive point, since it is the zodiacal midpoint of the October solar eclipse and the next solar eclipse on March 20, 2015. This two-eclipse midpoint is often a key factor in triggering changes in market trends.

Typically when we review these sensitive points in eclipse horoscopes, we look at the transiting dynamics in the fourth harmonic, which gives us conjunctions, oppositions, and squares to the degrees in question. In this case, however, in order to simplify our observations in a way that can make for more effective trading, our main concern is the first harmonic, so we have just listed the key conjunctions with sensitive points in the eclipse horoscope.

Although the eclipse we are considering doesn't take place until late October, we have also included the transits throughout September and October that can potentially activate the October 23 solar eclipse. Eclipses can cast significant shadows that trigger important events before the eclipses themselves actually occur, and we want to take that effect into account as we lead up to the date of the eclipse. Note as well that for a few months we have also included some of the key transits to the solar eclipse of April 2014, since that previous eclipse is still making its influence felt, although its effect is diminished.

In reviewing these dates for upcoming transits to sensitive points in eclipse horoscopes, pay particular attention to the "clusters" of eclipse activations, when several activations occur on the same day or within a period of two or three days. These occasions have a higher likelihood of being associated with significant geopolitical events, and can also bring extra energy to the market environment, amplifying market dynamics and increasing the potential for trend accelerations, break-outs, or reversals.

September 2, 2014	Mars conjunct October Eclipse Saturn
September 5, 2014	Venus opposition October Eclipse Antiscion
September 6, 2014	Sun opposition October Eclipse Chiron
September 9, 2014	Venus opposition October Eclipse Neptune
September 10, 2014	Mercury conjunct April Eclipse Mars
September 11, 2014	Mars opposition October Eclipse Admetos
September 11, 2014	Mercury opposition October Eclipse Uranus
September 12, 2014	April Eclipse Lunar Return
September 13, 2014	Mercury conjunct April Eclipse Zeus
September 14, 2014	Mercury conjunct October Eclipse Zeus
September 14, 2014	Mercury conjunct October Eclipse Mercury
September 16, 2014	Mercury conjunct True Lunar Node
September 16, 2014	Venus opposition October Eclipse Chiron
September 16, 2014	Hades conjunct October Eclipse Hades
September 22, 2014	True Node conjunct October Eclipse True Node
September 24, 2014	Kronos conjunct October Eclipse Kronos
September 24, 2014	Apollon conjunct April Eclipse Apollon
September 25, 2014	Mercury conjunct April Eclipse True Node
September 26, 2014	Mercury conjunct April Eclipse Apollon
September 27,2014	Mercury conjunct October Eclipse Apollon
September 27, 2014	Mercury conjunct October Eclipse Venus
September 28, 2014	Mercury conjunct October Eclipse Point
October 4, 2014	Saturn conjunct April Eclipse Saturn

October 5, 2014	Sun conjunct April Eclipse Mars
October 7, 2014	Saturn square April Eclipse Antiscion
October 7, 2014	Sun opposition October Eclipse Uranus
October 8, 2014	Sun conjunct April Eclipse Zeus
October 8, 2014	Total Lunar Eclipse
October 9, 2014	Venus conjunct April Eclipse Mars
October 9, 2014	April Eclipse Lunar Return
October 9, 2014	Sun conjunct October Eclipse Zeus
October 10, 2014	Mercury conjunct October Eclipse Point
October 10, 2014	Sun conjunct October Eclipse Mercury
October 10, 2014	Mercury conjunct October Eclipse Venus
October 10, 2014	Venus opposition October Eclipse Uranus
October 10, 2014	Mercury conjunct October Eclipse Apollon
October 11, 2014	Mercury conjunct April Eclipse Apollon
October 12, 2014	Venus conjunct April Eclipse Zeus
October 12, 2014	Mercury conjunct April Eclipse True Node
October 12, 2014	Sun conjunct October Eclipse True Lunar Node
October 12, 2014	Venus conjunct October Eclipse Zeus
October 13, 2014	Venus conjunct October Eclipse Mercury
October 15, 2014	Venus conjunct October Eclipse True Node
October 16, 2014	Mars conjunct October Eclipse Cupido
October 17, 2014	Poseidon conjunct April Eclipse Poseidon
October 18, 2014	Mars conjunct April Eclipse Cupido
October 20, 2014	Mercury conjunct October Eclipse True Node
October 21, 2014	Uranus conjunct April Eclipse Uranus
October 21, 2014	Sun conjunct April Eclipse True Node
October 22, 2014	Venus conjunct April Eclipse True Node
October 22, 2014	Sun conjunct April Eclipse Apollon
October 23, 2014	Venus conjunct April Eclipse Apollon
October 23, 2014	Sun conjunct October Eclipse Apollon
October 23, 2014	Sun conjunct October Eclipse Venus
October 23, 2014	Venus conjunct October Eclipse Apollon
October 23, 2014	Partial Solar Eclipse
October 24, 2014	Venus conjunct October Eclipse Point
October 27, 2014	Mercury conjunct October Eclipse Mercury
October 27, 2014	Venus square April/Oct 2-Eclipse Midpoint
October 27, 2014	Sun square April/Oct 2-Eclipse Midpoint
October 31, 2014	Mercury conjunct October Eclipse True Node

November 1, 2014	Venus conjunct April Eclipse Poseidon
November 1, 2014	Sun opposition April Eclipse Point
November 1, 2014	Mars opposition October Eclipse Hades
November 1, 2014	Venus conjunct October Eclipse Poseidon
November 2, 2014	Vulcanus conjunct October Eclipse Vulcanus
November 3, 2014	Sun conjunct April Eclipse Poseidon
November 3, 2014	Sun conjunct October Eclipse Poseidon
November 6, 2014	April Eclipse Lunar Return
November 7, 2014	Mercury conjunct April Eclipse True Node
November 7, 2014	Jupiter conjunct April Eclipse Antision
November 7, 2014	Mars opposition October Eclipse Kronos
November 8, 2014	Mercury conjunct April Eclipse Apollon
November 8, 2014	Mercury conjunct October Eclipse Apollon
November 8, 2014	Mercury conjunct October Eclipse Venus
November 9, 2014	Mercury conjunct October Eclipse Point
November 9, 2014	Venus conjunct April Eclipse Saturn
November 9, 2014	Venus square April Eclipse Antiscion
November 10, 2014	Mars conjunct October Eclipse Pluto
November 10, 2014	Apollon conjunct October Eclipse Venus
November 10, 2014	Venus conjunct October Eclipse Saturn
November 11, 2014	Mercury square April/Oct 2-Eclipse Midpoint
November 13, 2014	Sun conjunct April Eclipse Saturn
November 13, 2014	Mars conjunct April Eclipse Pluto
November 13, 2014	Sun square April Eclipse Antiscion
November 15, 2014	Mercury conjunct April Eclipse Poseidon
November 15, 2014	Mars conjunct Oct/March 2-Eclipse Midpoint
November 15, 2014	Sun conjunct October Eclipse Saturn
November 15, 2014	Venus opposition October Eclipse Admetos
November 15, 2014	Mercury conjunct October Eclipse Poseidon
November 20, 2014	October Eclipse Lunar Return
November 20, 2014	Sun opposition October Eclipse Admetos
November 22, 2014	Mercury conjunct April Eclipse Saturn
November 22, 2014	Mercury square April Eclipse Antiscion
November 23, 2014	Mercury conjunct October Eclipse Saturn
November 25, 2014	Zeus conjunct October Eclipse Mercury
November 27, 2014	Mercury opposition October Eclipse Admetos

December 3, 2014	April Eclipse Lunar Return
December 3, 2014	Mars opposition October Eclipse Vulcanus
December 4, 2014	Venus conjunct October Eclipse Cupido
December 5, 2014	Venus conjunct April Eclipse Cupido
December 7, 2014	Apollon conjunct October Eclipse Point
December 8, 2014	Neptune conjunct October Eclipse Neptune
December 9, 2014	Venus conjunct October Eclipse Mars
December 10, 2014	True Node conjunct October Eclipse Mercury
December 10, 2014	Mars opposition April/Oct 2-Eclipse Midpoint
December 12, 2014	Saturn opposition October Eclipse Admetos
December 12, 2014	Mercury conjunct October Eclipse Cupido
December 13, 2014	Mercury conjunct April Eclipse Cupido
December 14, 2014	Venus opposition October Eclipse Hades
December 14, 2014	Sun conjunct October Eclipse Cupido
December 15, 2014	Sun conjunct April Eclipse Cupido
December 15, 2014	Mercury conjunct October Eclipse Mars
December 17, 2014	October Eclipse Lunar Return
December 17, 2014	Venus opposition October Eclipse Kronos
December 19, 2014	Venus conjunct October Eclipse Pluto
December 19, 2014	Mercury opposition October Eclipse Hades
December 19, 2014	Sun conjunct October Eclipse Mars
December 20, 2014	Cupido conjunct April Eclipse Cupido
December 20, 2014	True Lunar Node conjunct October Eclipse Zeus
December 21, 2014	Venus conjunct April Eclipse Pluto
December 22, 2014	Venus conjunct Oct/March 2-Eclipse Midpoint
December 22, 2014	Mercury opposition October Eclipse Kronos
December 24, 2014	Mercury conjunct October Eclipse Pluto
December 24, 2014	Chiron conjunct October Eclipse Chiron
December 25, 2014	Mercury conjunct April Eclipse Pluto
December 26, 2014	True Node conjunct April Eclipse Zeus
December 26, 2014	Sun opposition October Eclipse Hades
December 26, 2014	Mercury conjunct Oct/March 2-Eclipse Midpoint
December 29, 2014	Mars opposition October Eclipse Jupiter
December 30, 2014	April Eclipse Lunar Return
December 30, 2014	Sun opposition October Eclipse Kronos
January 1, 2015	Sun conjunct October Eclipse Pluto
January 2, 2015	Venus opposition October Eclipse Vulcanus

January 4, 2015	Mercury opposition October Eclipse Vulcanus
January 5, 2015	Sun conjunct Oct/March 2-Eclipse Midpoint
January 8, 2015	True Node opposition October Eclipse Uranus
January 11, 2015	Mars conjunct October Eclipse Antiscion
January 13, 2015	October Eclipse Lunar Return
January 18, 2015	Mars conjunct October Eclipse Neptune
January 18, 2015	Venus opposition October Eclipse Jupiter
January 19, 2015	Sun opposition October Eclipse Vulcanus
January 20, 2015	Sun square October Eclipse Point
January 23, 2015	Jupiter conjunct October Eclipse Jupiter
January 27, 2015	Venus conjunct October Eclipse Antiscion
January 29, 2015	Mars conjunct October Eclipse Chiron
January 31, 2015	Venus conjunct October Eclipse Neptune
February 7, 2015	Venus conjunct October Eclipse Chiron
February 8, 2015	Sun opposition October Eclipse Jupiter
February 10, 2015	October Eclipse Lunar Return
February 16, 2015	Uranus conjunct October Eclipse Uranus
February 18, 2015	Sun conjunct October Eclipse Antiscion
February 23, 2015	Sun conjunct October Eclipse Neptune
February 26, 2015	Pluto conjunct Oct/March 2-Eclipse Midpoint
March 3, 2015	Venus conjunct October Eclipse Uranus
March 4, 2015	Sun conjunct October Eclipse Chiron
March 5, 2015	Mercury opposition October Eclipse Jupiter
March 6, 2015	Venus opposition October Eclipse Zeus
March 6, 2015	Venus opposition October Eclipse Mercury
March 8, 2015	Venus opposition October Eclipse True Node
March 9, 2015	October Eclipse Lunar Return
March 10, 2015	Mars conjunct October Eclipse Uranus
March 10, 2015	Zeus conjunct October Eclipse Mercury
March 12, 2015	Mercury conjunct October Eclipse Antiscion
March 13, 2015	Mars opposition October Eclipse Zeus
March 14, 2015	Mars opposition October Eclipse Mercury
March 16, 2015	Mercury conjunct October Eclipse Neptune
March 17, 2015	Venus opposition October Eclipse Apollon
March 17, 2015	Mars opposition October Eclipse True Lunar Node
March 17, 2015	Venus opposition October Eclipse Venus

March 17, 2015	Venus opposition October Eclipse Point
March 20, 2015	Total Solar Eclipse
March 21, 2015	Mercury conjunct October Eclipse Chiron
March 23, 2015	Apollon conjunct October Eclipse Point
March 26, 2015	Venus opposition October Eclipse Poseidon
March 31, 2015	Mars opposition October Eclipse Apollon
March 31, 2015	Mars opposition October Eclipse Venus
April 1, 2015	Mars opposition October Eclipse Point
April 3, 2015	Sun conjunct October Eclipse Uranus
April 4, 2015	Total Lunar Eclipse
April 5, 2015	Venus opposition October Eclipse Saturn
April 5, 2015	October Eclipse Lunar Return
April 6, 2015	Sun opposition October Eclipse Zeus
April 7, 2015	Mercury conjunct October Eclipse Uranus
April 7, 2015	Sun opposition October Eclipse Mercury
April 8, 2015	Mercury opposition October Eclipse Zeus
April 8, 2015	Uranus opposition October Eclipse Zeus
April 8, 2015	Mercury opposition October Eclipse Mercury
April 9, 2015	Sun opposition October Eclipse True Node
April 9, 2015	Mercury opposition October Eclipse True Node
April 10, 2015	Venus conjunct October Eclipse Admetos
April 14, 2015	Mercury opposition October Eclipse Apollon
April 14, 2015	Mercury opposition October Eclipse Venus
April 14, 2015	Mercury opposition October Eclipse Point
April 15, 2015	Mars opposition October Eclipse Poseidon
April 16, 2015	Zeus conjunct October Eclipse Zeus
April 17, 2015	Uranus opposition October Eclipse Mercury
April 20, 2015	Sun opposition October Eclipse Apollon
April 20, 2015	Mercury opposition October Eclipse Poseidon
April 20, 2015	Sun opposition October Eclipse Venus
April 20, 2015	Sun opposition October Eclipse Point
April 22, 2015	Apollon conjunct October Eclipse Venus
April 26, 2015	Mercury opposition October Eclipse Saturn
April 30, 2015	Mercury conjunct October Eclipse Admetos
May 1, 2015	Venus opposition October Eclipse Cupido
May 1, 2015	Sun opposition October Eclipse Poseidon

May 2, 2015	Mars opposition October Eclipse Saturn
May 2, 2015	October Eclipse Lunar Return
May 6, 2015	Venus opposition October Eclipse Mars
May 10, 2015	Mars conjunct October Eclipse Admetos
May 11, 2015	Venus conjunct October Eclipse Hades
May 13, 2015	Sun opposition October Eclipse Saturn
May 15, 2015	Apollon conjunct October Eclipse Apollon
May 16, 2015	Venus conjunct October Eclipse Kronos
May 18, 2015	Venus opposition October Eclipse Pluto
May 19, 2015	Sun conjunct October Eclipse Admetos
May 21, 2015	Venus opposition Oct/March 2-Eclipse Midpoint
May 22, 2015	Admetos conjunct October Eclipse Admetos
May 31, 2015	Uranus opposition October Eclipse True Node

Eclipse Trading Opportunities

While it's interesting to review the history of past eclipses and to speculate about the overall impact that the eclipse of October 23, 2014 will have on the market in general, it's also useful to identify specific trading opportunities in individual equities that are linked to the eclipse.

In reviewing potential candidates for eclipse related trades, we are first of all concerned with identifying those stocks whose First-Trade horoscopes are significantly impacted by the eclipse itself. When a solar eclipse conjoins the First-Trade Sun or the First-Trade Midheaven, experience has shown that we are more likely to see that particular stock appreciate in value during the months following the eclipse.

In some cases, there will be an opportunity to take profits in these stocks when the Sun squares the eclipse point or when it conjoins the two-eclipse midpoint. In cases where the trade has turned profitable, however, it may be advisable to take some money off the table at one or both of those occasions, while leaving a portion of the position open for possible future price appreciation. That kind of decision, of course, is left up to the discretion of the individual astro-trader.

It's important to note that an activation of the First-Trade horoscope by a solar eclipse is not sufficient in and of itself to warrant indiscriminate buying of the stock. In all of our stock selections we are concerned not only about the astrological dynamics at work, but also about corporate fundamentals and about the technical picture presented by the stock's trading history. When an eclipse activates significant planetary pictures or midpoint structures in the First-Trade horoscope, we are far more likely to consider that stock as a possible trading candidate.

Here are four individual stocks that offer some potential for price appreciation following the solar eclipse on October 23, 2014. In each case, our trading strategy will be to put on a long position soon after the eclipse takes place. This is typically within a couple of weeks following the eclipse (in some cases waiting for price pull-backs where appropriate for optimum purchasing opportunities).

Our plan is to set an initial stop on each trade to minimize risk exposure, to trail a stop if a trade turns profitable, and then, if we are still in the trade, to reevaluate our positions around January 5, 2015, when we will get the Sun's conjunction with the October/March two-eclipse midpoint, and on January 20, 2015, when the transiting Sun squares the October Eclipse Point.

China Mobile Limited (NYSE - CHL)

An investment holding company offering mobile telecommunications and related services in Mainland China and Hong Kong, China Mobile Limited provides voice services and voice value-added services as well as data services, including both SMS and MMS messaging. In addition, it provides wireless data traffic services comprising mobile data traffic and WLAN data traffic; and applications and information services, including mobile music, mobile paper, mobile reading, mobile video, mobile market, etc. Further, the company offers telecommunications network planning design and consulting services; roaming clearance services; technology platform development and maintenance services; and mobile data solutions, system integration, and development, as well as operates a network and business coordination center. Additionally, it is involved in network planning and optimizing construction testing and supervising activities; technology support; development and training of Nokia GSM900/1800 mobile communication system; designing and selling electronic communication products; and provision of non-banking financial services. Formerly known as China Mobile (Hong Kong) Limited, it changed its name to China Mobile Limited in May 2006. Incorporated in 1997 and based in Central, Hong Kong, China Mobile Limited is a subsidiary of China Mobile Hong Kong (BVI) Limited. The planetary price lines in our trading chart are for geocentric Venus and Hades in the eighth harmonic.

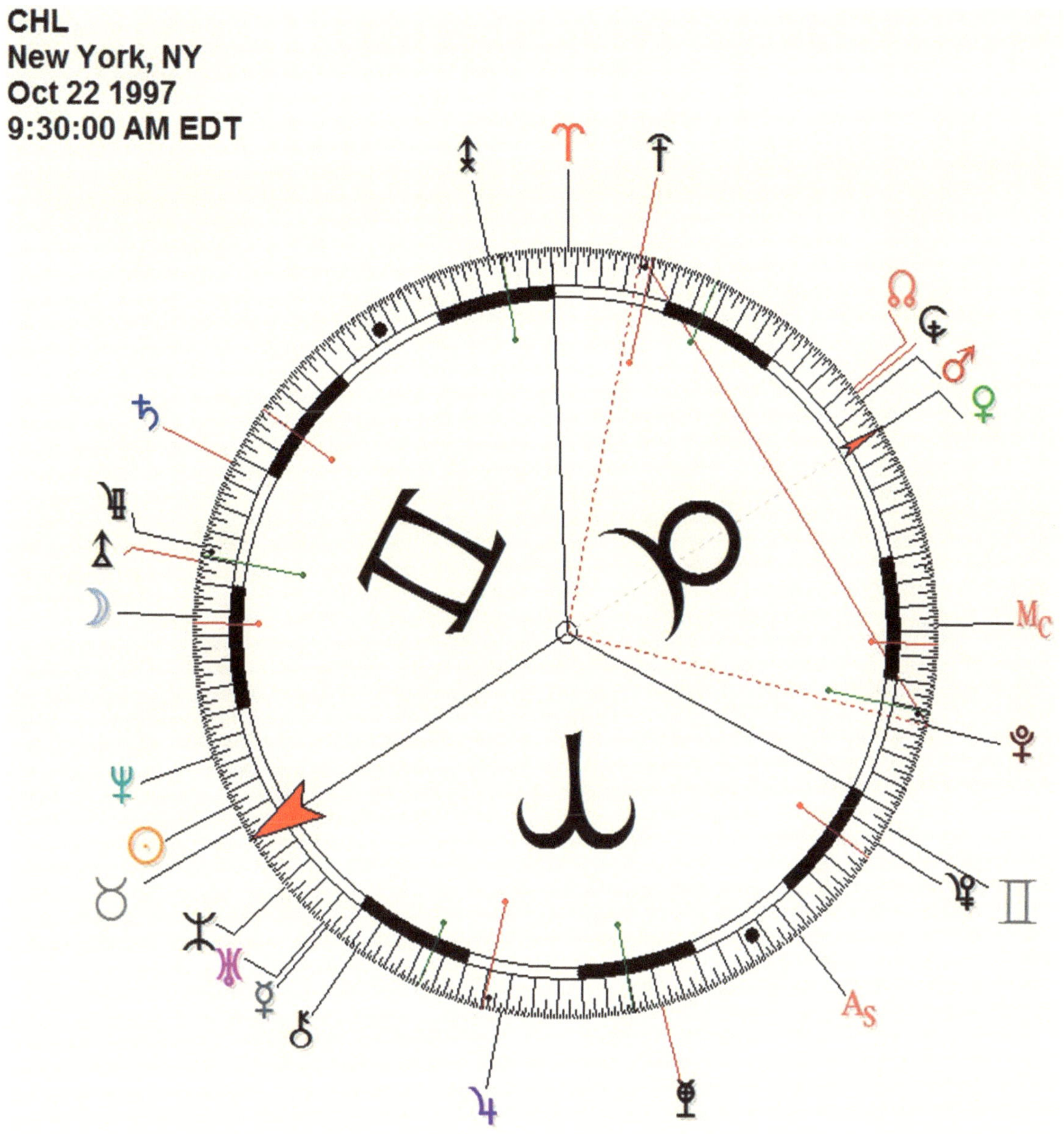

The October partial solar eclipse activates the Sun and Venus (which is semi-square the Sun) in the CHL First-Trade horoscope, as well as the powerful Pluto/Kronos midpoint.

Minerals Technologies Inc. (NYSE - MTX)

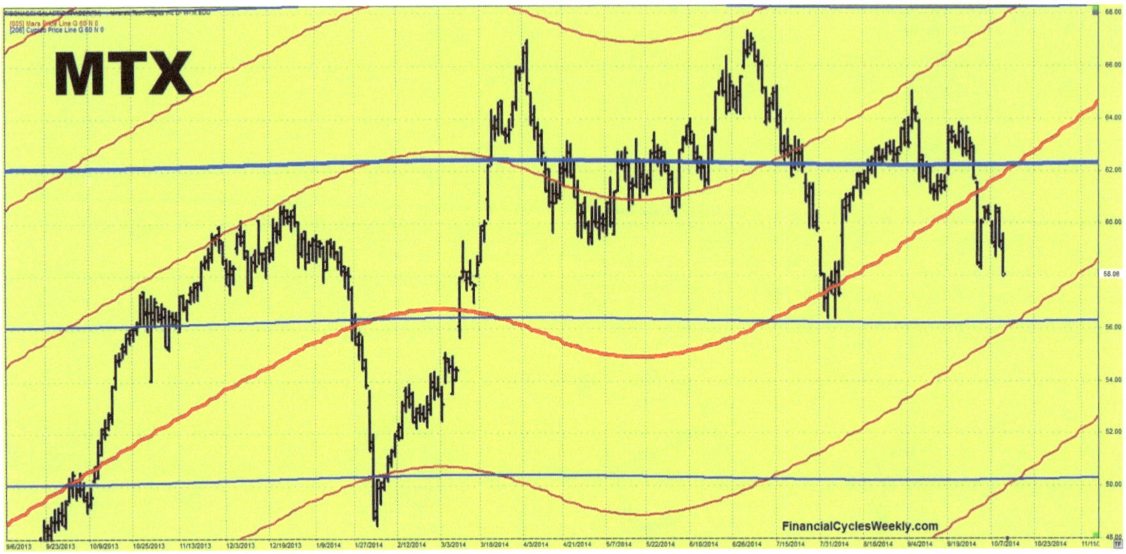

Minerals Technologies Inc., a resource and technology based company, develops, produces, and markets various specialty mineral, mineral-based, and synthetic mineral products, and supporting systems and services worldwide. The company operates through two segments, Specialty Minerals and Refractories. The Specialty Minerals segment produces and sells synthetic mineral product precipitated calcium carbonate; and processed mineral product quicklime. It also mines mineral ores; and processes and sells natural mineral products, primarily limestone and talc. This segment's products are used in the paper, building materials, paint and coatings, glass, ceramic, polymer, food, automotive, and pharmaceutical industries. The Refractories segment produces and markets monolithic and shaped refractory materials and specialty products, services, and application and measurement equipment, and calcium metal and metallurgical wire products that are primarily used in high-temperature applications in the steel, non-ferrous metal, and glass industries. The company markets its products primarily through its direct sales force, as well as regional distributors. Minerals Technologies Inc. was founded in 1968 and is headquartered in New York, New York. In tracking the price action for this stock with planetary price lines, we're using geocentric Mars and Cupido in the sixth harmonic.

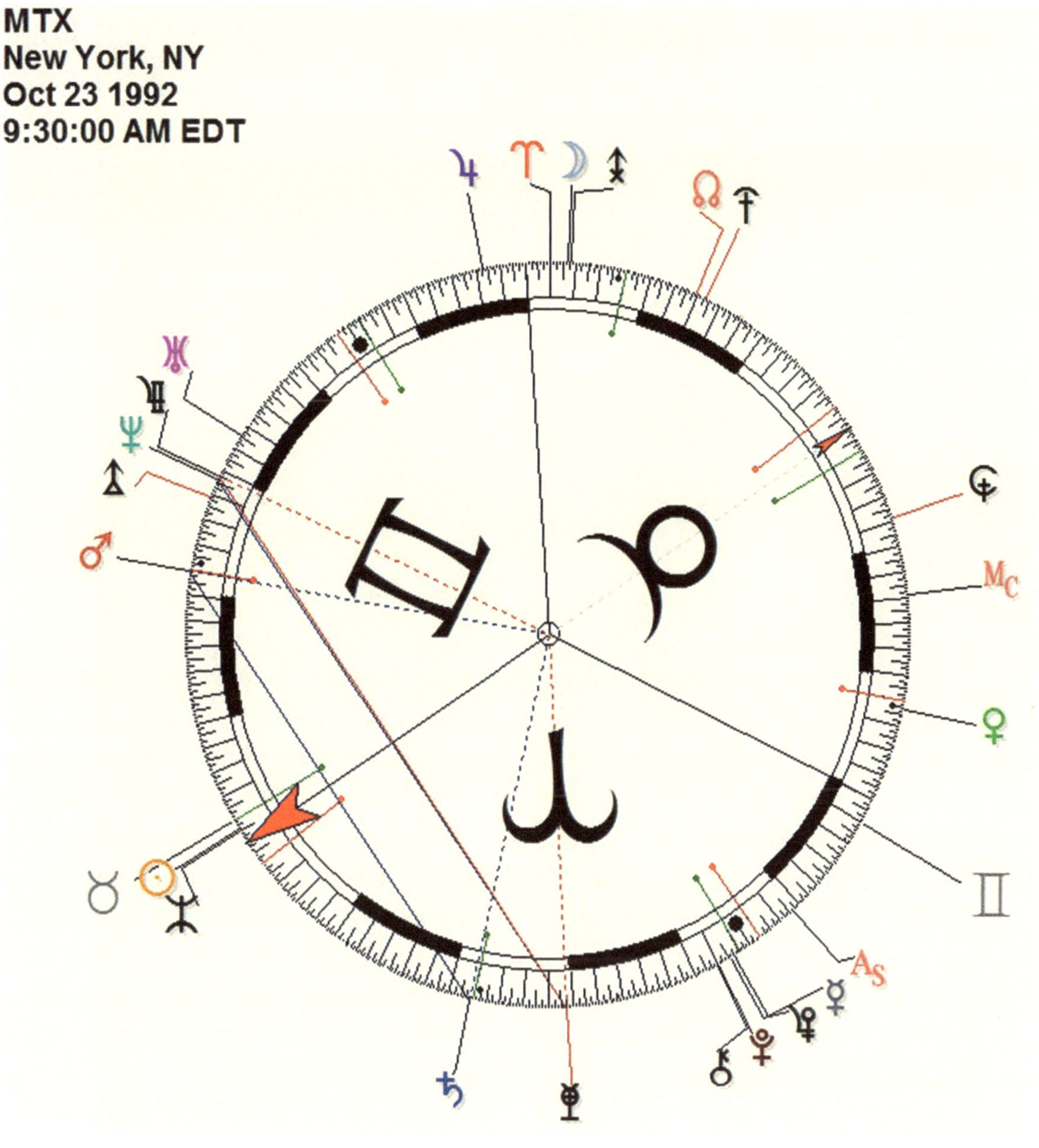

The solar eclipse in October activates the Sun and Poseidon, along with the midpoints for Mars/Saturn, Neptune/Admetos, and Apollon/Admetos in the MTX First-Trade horoscope.

Old Dominion Freight Line Inc. (NASDAQ - ODFL)

Old Dominion Freight Line, Inc. operates as a less-than-truckload (LTL) motor carrier in North America. It provides regional, inter-regional, and national LTL services; and other logistics services. The company also offers various value-added services, including international freight forwarding, ground and air expedited transportation, container delivery, truckload brokerage, supply chain consulting, warehousing, and consumer household pickup and delivery. As of December 31, 2013, it owned 6,296 tractors and 25,052 trailers, as well as operated 221 service centers. The company was founded in 1934 and is based in Thomasville, North Carolina. The trading action in ODFL resonates with geocentric planetary price lines for Mars and Neptune in the sixteenth harmonic.

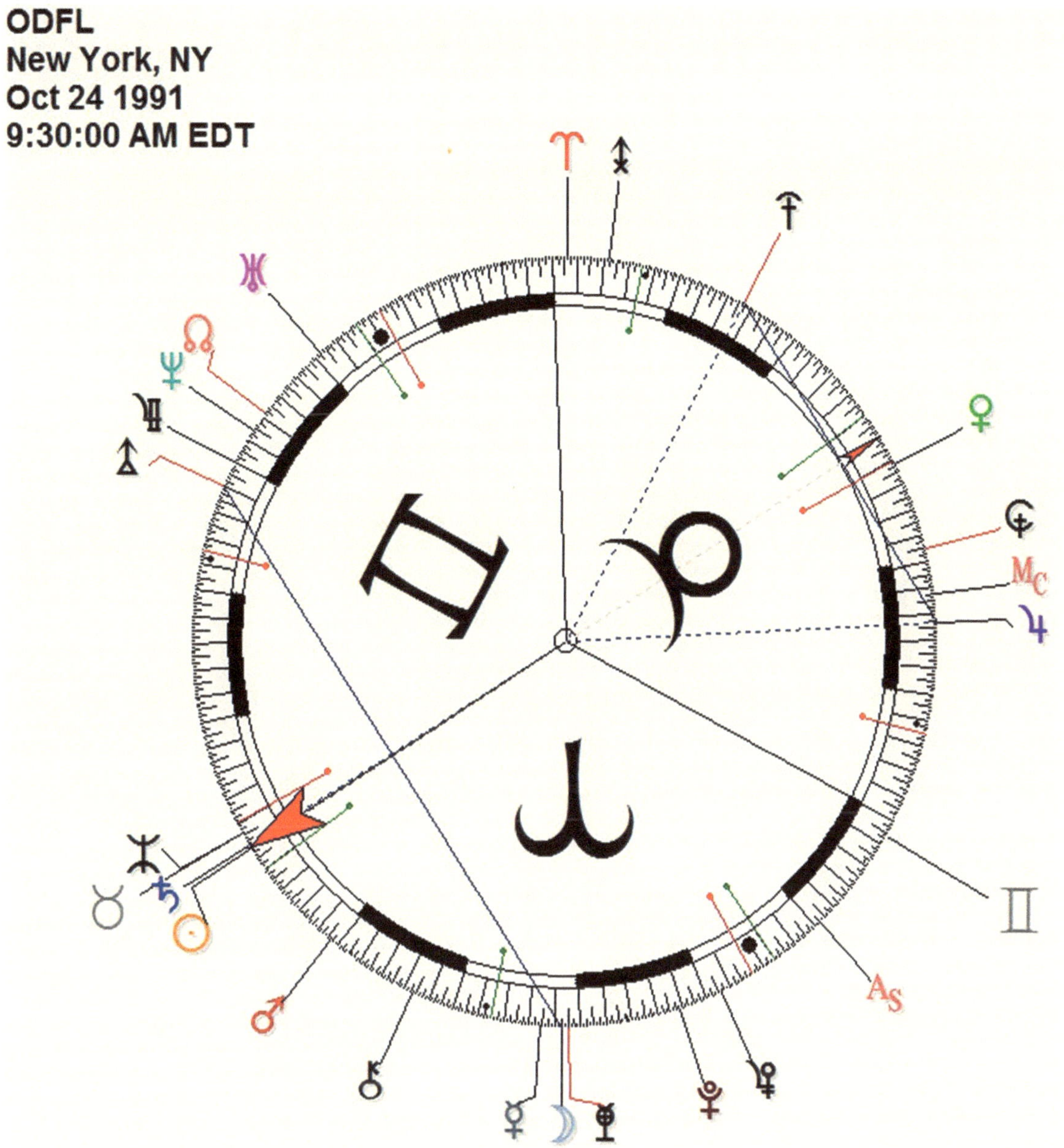

The ODFL First-Trade horoscope picks up the October solar eclipse effects through the Sun, Venus, and Saturn as well as the Sun/Saturn, Moon/Vulcanus, and Jupiter/Krons midpoints.

Principal Financial Group Inc. (NYSE – PFG)

Principal Financial Group, Inc. provides retirement savings, investment, and insurance products and services. Its Retirement and Investor Services provides products and services for retirement savings and investment to businesses, institutional clients, and individuals. The Principal Global Investors segment provides equity, fixed income, real estate, and other alternative investments, as well as currency management, asset allocation, stable value management, and other structured investment strategies. The Principal International segment offers retirement products and services and other financial products in Brazil, Chile, China, Hong Kong, India, Mexico, and Southeast Asia. The U.S. Insurance Solutions segment provides individual life insurance products as well as specialty benefits consisting of group dental and vision insurance, individual and group disability insurance, and group life insurance, as well as non-medical fee-for-service claims administration services in the United States. Principal Financial Group, Inc. was founded in 1879 and is headquartered in Des Moines, Iowa. We track its trading with geocentric sixth-harmonic price lines for Venus and Jupiter.

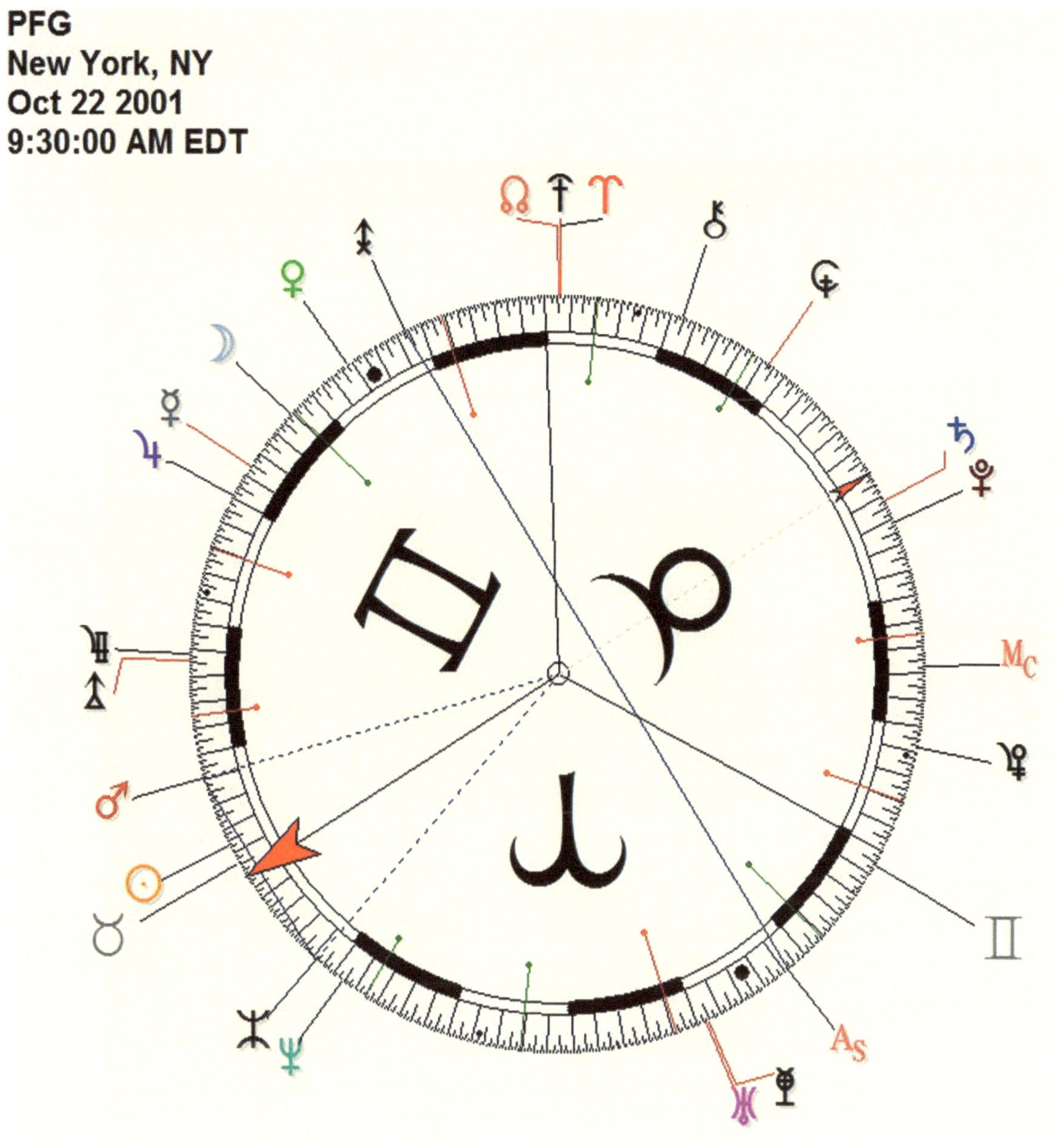

The October solar eclipse triggers the PFG First-Trade Sun and Saturn, along with the First-Trade Mars/Poseidon and Zeus/Ascendant midpoints.

DISCLAIMER

The Solar Eclipse of October 2014: Its Impact on the Markets is a general interest publication which has been prepared from astrological information, news reports, cycle projections, and market observations which are believed to be accurate and reliable, but which cannot be guaranteed. Even with accurate information, past performance is no guarantee of future results. Speculation in securities and commodities involves considerable financial risk, and readers who plan to invest or speculate in securities or commodities mentioned in ***The Solar Eclipse of October 2014: Its Impact on the Markets*** have the complete personal responsibility for making themselves fully aware of all the risks involved before they invest. The authors of this report may at various times have positions in the securities and commodities discussed in this publication, and the information in ***The Solar Eclipse of October 2014: Its Impact on the Markets*** should in no way be understood or construed as a solicitation or an offer to buy or sell any products or securities, nor should the material published herein be considered buy/sell advice.

About the Authors

In 1993 Paul Farrell's book Think Astrology & Grow Rich highlighted **Tim Bost** as a pioneer in what *Business Week* called "the dawning of the Age of Financial Astrology."

Since that time, Tim has gained an international reputation as one of the most innovative thinkers and insightful teachers in financial astrology today. His email newsletter, FinancialCyclesWeekly.com, is eagerly read by traders, investors, and astrologers around the world, and is often cited in BARRON'S and other mainstream financial publications.

Tim has appeared frequently as a featured guest on Michael Yorba's Commodities Classics trading show on yorba.tv, and as a regular guest commentator on the Traders Network radio show on the Clear Channel Network. His trading articles are featured on the TraderPlanet.com website and in ***Traders World*** magazine. He has also been a regular contributor to the ***Traders' Astrological Almanac*** for nearly two decades. His Basic Stock Market Astrology Home Study Course has helped students from all backgrounds get started in profitable astro-trading. He has had a wide and enthusiastic response to his books, monographs and recorded lectures, including "Mercury, Money and the Markets," "How to Find the Money in Your Horoscope," "Beyond Symbolism in Financial Astrology," "How to Become a Stock Market Lunatic," "How You can Profit from the Billionaire's Secret," "Creating Personal Wealth with Astrology," "The Planetary Station Super-Cluster," "Gann Secrets Revealed," "Uranus & Hades: Obscene Corruption & Speculative Surprises," "Beyond the Basics in Stock Market Astrology," "Mars/Pluto Market Activations 2012-2025," "8 Billionaire Strategies for Breakthrough Stock Market Success," and many other titles.

A native of North Carolina with over 40 years of experience in astrology, Tim Bost has lived in the Sarasota, Florida area since 1996. He has earned the highest levels of certification from several professional associations, including the ISAR Certified Astrological Professional designation, the NCGR Level 4 certification, and the professional level certification from the American Federation of Astrologers.

Tim works in person and by telephone with businesses and individual clients throughout the world, providing astrological insights, counseling, and coaching services to CEOs, entrepreneurs, professionals, money managers, traders, and investors. His program on Rapid Astro-Trading Mastery is designed to transform the trading results of individual traders; his newest instructional program, "How To Find The Money In Your Horoscope," provides tools and techniques for in-depth financial analysis of the natal chart.

To get Tim Bost's latest comments on the markets, current astrological applications, and the astro-trading advantage, be sure to visit his personal blog at http://realbusinessresults.com/marketastrologer

Jim Cummins has also been a professional astrologer for more than 40 years. His work has been primarily in teaching, and in private consultations. His clients, individual and corporate, are from every continent, and many of his students have become successful astrologers in their own right.

As an astrologer, and as a musician, Jim has traveled the globe, teaching astrology; appearing on various radio and TV programs both in the U.S. and Europe, frequently contributing articles on astrology for the local press wherever he was; serving individual clients; and performing as pianist in hotels and on cruise ships.

Jim and his wife Joyce currently reside in Central Florida, where, for many months, he wrote the Astrologer-at-Large column in the internationally distributed bi-weekly, *Pasco Naturally*; and authored a regularly featured astrological analysis of world events for the prestigious Norwegian astrology magazine, *Zodiac*, where his articles were translated into Norwegian for publication and distribution throughout northern Europe, especially the Nordic countries.

Jim currently serves as President of the Astrology Association of St. Petersburg, Florida. He can be reached through Tim Bost at Financial Cycles Weekly.

www.ingramcontent.com/pod-product-compliance
Lightning Source LLC
Chambersburg PA
CBHW041321210926
51847CB00002B/16
9781933198507